WHAT PEOPLE A

CAPTURED BY GRACE...

If you've ever wondered why your Christian life isn't as thrilling as it should be, this book is for you. In *Captured by Grace*, Ben Dailey is raw, real, and unfiltered. He shares his own struggle to find the truth and shows us how to take a deep dive into God's grace like never before. Here, you'll find unexpected encouragement, unwavering confidence with God, and a rock-solid stability in Jesus you never dreamed possible.

Dr. Andrew Farley
Bestselling author, national radio host, and speaker at
AndrewFarley.org
Lubbock, Texas

Pastor Ben Dailey understands that the church is not a health club for workout junkies; it's a rehab center for those wanting to be weaned off empty religion. If you're addicted to self-improvement, or if you are entangled in guilt and shame, the message of this book will set you free. Some truth is better felt than telt, and in this book you will feel the strong and liberating embrace of your heavenly Father. Relax, breathe, and allow yourself to be captured by grace.

Dr. Paul Ellis
Author of *Letters from Jesus*
Aukland, New Zealand

It has been said that only a changed man can change another man. Ben Dailey is such a man—one transformed by the gospel of grace and fully equipped to use his past to fertilize another man's future. He came through the years of grace-deprived ministry and now writes with the tenderness and compassion of one who has experienced both. His new book reflects that transformation and is sure to be a breath of fresh air to all who read it.

Paul White
Author of *Revelation To Transformation*
Flowery Branch, Georgia

I have known Ben Dailey for decades, and I have observed his transformation and his development from a young intern to a senior leader with national influence. I'm most impressed with his development of LANGUAGE that helps him clearly articulate a biblical truth that has been seen but not received, heard but not internalized, expounded often but many times without insight. His ability to bring freedom to people who have had a God-moment but are still in bondage is insightful and life-changing. No one in the family of God should feel like they are trapped by their past, shadowed by shame and guilt, or bound by judgmental theology. This book is an eye opener, a myth buster, a direct hit against wrong beliefs that keep us working for something that has already been paid for.

Maury Davis
Coach, consultant, pastor, teacher, and author of *10 Mistakes*,
MauryDavis.com
Nashville, Tennessee

The most effective teachers make complex things simple, and Ben Dailey delivers just that in *Captured by Grace*. Wherever you are on your spiritual journey, this book provides waves of clarity. A fresh revelation of the gospel has never been more needed than right now.

Greg Ford
Lead Pastor of One Church, www.one.church
Gahanna, Ohio

If you are fortunate enough to be holding this book in your hands, don't put it down! In it you will find truth that will set you free! Ben Dailey is a leading voice in a long-overdue movement of re-discovering the power of the Gospel as God originally delivered it. The moment you finally settle the issue of God's irrevocable faithfulness to you is the moment your fears will begin to fade. This book will lead you there!

Jeremy White
Pastor, speaker, and author of *The Gospel Uncut*
Vacaville, California

Congratulations! You are about to be seriously blessed by reading this book. I certainly was! Pastor Ben teaches the message of grace, a.k.a., the true Gospel, with contagious conviction and persistent passion! It's not just a message he teaches . . . it's the life he lives and models to his family, friends, and church. I have the great honor and pleasure of knowing Pastor Ben as a great friend and co-laborer in the Lord. He is a true gift to his thriving church, Calvary, as well as the entire body of Christ! Listen, I am so confident that *Captured by Grace* will change your life that I'll personally offer you my own "money back guarantee" on this book! (Seriously, if this book doesn't bring you into a deeper knowledge of God's love, contact me, and I'll pay for the book, no strings attached. That's how convinced I am of the power of this book!). Now, open your heart and get ready to experience a new level of freedom in Christ, because you are about to be captured by His grace!

Ashley Terradez
President & Founder of Terradez Ministries & Global Church Family
Colorado Springs, Colorado

Grace is something I think many people misunderstand—or at least miss having a full understanding of. With this book, Ben Dailey makes it something we can all understand more fully and allow it to capture us completely. *Captured by Grace* is a book you'll want to keep within arm's reach for a long time.

Dino Rizzo
Executive Director, ARC (Association of Related Churches)
Associate Pastor, Church of the Highlands
Birmingham, Alabama

In *Captured by Grace*, Pastor Ben Dailey celebrates the powerful liberty of the limitless provision of grace in Christ Jesus! By sharing his personal journey that was hindered by years of legalism and moralism, he discovered that he suffered from PTRSD, "Post Traumatic Religious Stress Syndrome," but he began to experience the grace of God that empowers a life full of liberty, joy, and love in Christ! This transformation begins from the inside out so that we can live the full and free life Christ died to provide. This book affirms Christ's fulfillment of the legal requirements for salvation and liberates the reader from a performance-driven Christian life! As Ben states, "Christ's grace gives us the power to live, really live!" Christ has more for us than the crushing grind of self-effort! When you read, *Captured by Grace,* you will find out that GOD HAS MUCH MORE FOR YOU THAN THAT!" This is a book well worth the reading!

Dr. Gaylan D. Claunch
Superintendent, North Texas District of the Assembly of God
Waxahachie, Texas

My friend, Ben Dailey, has taken us on a journey that integrates biblical truth (theology) with every day, practical living (application). Penetrating insights search through the rubble of our broken lives, rescuing us from the effects of faulty foundations built on religious ideology that has never experienced the life-giving realities of the bloody cross and the empty tomb! As a practitioner, Ben does not specialize in theory, but in the power of the Gospel that has resulted in the most amazing, transformed lives. People who were once "dead" ... are now FULLY ALIVE! I encourage you to dive in! These truths are not specialized to certain cultures, genders, or ethnicities. This book will awaken life inside any person who wants to live life till it overflows. When you step in, you will find that you've been "captured" by love that is divine!

Bishop Tony Miller
Destiny Fellowship of Churches and Ministries
Oklahoma City, Oklahoma

CAPTURED BY

GRACE

BE FREED FROM FEAR SO YOU CAN REALLY LIVE!

BEN DAILEY

ISBNs:
Print: 978-1-947505-30-8
Ebook versions: 978-1-947505-31-5

Cover concept by Juniper + Co., Irving, Texas (Juniperco.art)
Interior formatting by Anne McLaughlin, Blue Lake Design
Published by Baxter Press, Friendswood, Texas

Printed in the United States

DEDICATION

God has demonstrated His grace to me through a number of
people, and I want to dedicate this book to them.
They live what this book is about.

Kim, because of you, my eyes were opened to grace,
and because of you, I've had the courage to continue in grace.

Kyla and Kade, both of you have patiently journeyed with me
as God has opened my eyes more fully to His grace,
and you've loved me unconditionally.

The entire Calvary Church family, you've loved me, encouraged
me, and challenged me to craft the message of this book. I have by
no means arrived, but I've at least made a good start!

Pete Briscoe, a butcher cuts to hurt and a surgeon cuts to heal,
and you've been a spiritual surgeon to me. You've cut me open and
lovingly dealt with the deep wounds and spiritual tumors you've
found there. You've walked with me through a deep renewal
process that has forever impacted my heart and life.

Paul Ellis, I've learned so much from you. In a way, learning the
new covenant is learning an entirely new language. You've been
my long-distance teacher, expanding my grace vocabulary and
teaching me the sentence structure of God's redeeming truth.

CONTENTS

I was captured by grace, so that Jesus Christ could display
through me the outpouring of his Spirit
as a pattern to be seen for all those
who would believe in him for eternal life.

1 Timothy 1:16 The Passion Translation

FOREWORD

When the angel of the Lord appeared to Mary, He said to her, "Hail, you are highly favored and blessed among women." She cast in her mind what manner of salutation this was. Perhaps she was astonished because she wasn't accustomed to hearing good news. As you read the pages of this book, this may well be your first reaction, too. Rest assured: the gospel really is Good News, even if you aren't accustomed to hearing it. Many times, we who preach the gospel of grace get accused of being feel-good preachers, to which I reply, "That's why it's called the good news!" You should leave church feeling better than you did before you came.

For some reason, people find it easier to believe the bad news that brings fear and condemnation than the edifying good news of God's amazing grace. I'm reminded of the story of Joshua and Caleb, the two spies who came back with a good report after spying out the Promised Land. They didn't join the majority who declared the popular message of bad news. It always amazes me that the people wanted to stone the men carrying the good news, while at the same time, celebrating the bearers of bad news. Instead, we should celebrate men like Ben Dailey who have the courage to preach good news and be a part of a gospel revolution. I'm proud to call him my friend and co-laborer in the gospel of grace.

Perhaps you are like Mary. You are hearing the message of being highly favored and your response is like Mary's—you aren't used to hearing good news. Her response was, "How can this be?" The angel's answer was, "The Holy Ghost will overshadow you and the power of the highest will come upon you." Ben Dailey, in this incredible treatise of New Covenant truth, is delivering just such a message. You are highly favored, deeply loved, and accepted in the Beloved. This book may well be your first step in recovering from, as Ben calls it in his first chapter, "post-traumatic religious stress disorder—PTRSD." I pray that as you read this book, the Holy Spirit will overshadow you and the power of the highest will come upon you to confirm how Abba truly feels about you.

Knowing you are loved and accepted as a son or daughter is one of the most empowering truths you will ever experience. To the thirsty heart, this book is a refreshing drink of living water. Get ready to recover your life.

Dr. Lynn Hiles
Author and host of the internationally broadcast television program,
Dr. Lynn Hiles, That You Might Have Life
Berkeley Springs, West Virginia

CHAPTER 1

THE WAR IS OVER!

DECEPTION VS. TRUTH

IN THE SUMMER OF 1945, THE WAR IN EUROPE HAD ENDED IN THE
defeat of Germany and Italy, but fierce fighting continued on the islands
of the South Pacific between the proud Japanese and the Allied forces.[1] Japanese soldiers had pledged their lives to Emperor Hirohito, and
very few surrendered, even after devastating defeats on the battlefields.
As the Allies made progress by taking island after island, American
and British commanders prepared for an invasion of Japan's home islands. The Japanese had kept their most formidable armies to defend
the homeland. Some experts predicted a million Allied casualties, and
many more killed and wounded Japanese soldiers and civilians. When
the war suddenly ended in August after two atomic bombs, the armed
forces and civilians on the two sides had opposite reactions: The Allies erupted in jubilant celebration, but the Japanese were incredulous.
They had been told they were winning the war, and they couldn't imagine the reality of defeat. Even the Emperor's voice over the radio telling

the people of the surrender was a surreal experience for the Japanese forces and civilians—they had never heard his voice before, and countless thousands had given their lives for him.

Gradually, the truth of the surrender erased the false hopes of Japanese victory, and millions of soldiers put down their rifles and went home to their families. Japanese forces were scattered throughout the islands of the Pacific, and it took days or even weeks for all of them to hear the news. Even then, one man remained sure the announcement of Japan's defeat was only an Allied ruse to get their soldiers to expose themselves. Lieutenant Hiroo Onoda refused to come out.

In 1944 as the Allies slowly drew closer to Japan, Onoda had been ordered to serve as an intelligence officer on the Philippine island of Lubang to sabotage the harbor and airstrip as the Allies advanced. When he arrived, however, his commanding officer issued different orders: assist with the Japanese evacuation as the Allies came ashore and stay after virtually everyone else had gone. The major told him, "It may take three years, it may take five, but whatever happens, we'll come back for you."[2]

Months later, the war ended, but no one had come back to Onoda. His fellow soldiers told the authorities that he was still in the Philippine jungle, so they dropped leaflets from planes to convince him. It didn't work. In fact, nothing worked. For twenty-nine years, Onoda stayed in the jungle even though the war had long been over and Japan was flourishing again.

In 1974, a Japanese college student found Onoda and tried to explain that the announcement almost three decades before wasn't a trick, but the old soldier still refused to come out. Finally, the Japanese government sent Onoda's former commander, the major, into the jungle to order him to surrender and return to Japan. It had been easy to dismiss broadcasts, leaflets, and a college student, but he couldn't disobey a direct order from his commanding officer. For Onoda, the war was finally over.

What does Lieutenant Onoda's story have to do with living the Christian life? Everything! Many Christians are just like Lieutenant Onoda—the war is over, but we refuse to believe it. We continue to live in a jungle of doubts and fears. In fact, when we hear the glorious message of God's grace that has freed us from sin and empowers us to live the Christ-life every day, we resist the idea. It just can't be true! It's a ruse to trick us! Instead, we remain loyal to the old regime of legalism, moralism, and performance to earn acceptance, but even our best efforts are never enough. The jungle of guilt and shame (when we fail) or arrogance (when we perform better than someone else) is a harsh and unforgiving place. There, we starve because merely following rules leaves our souls famished, we become enslaved to routines or we give up and walk away from the faith, and we compete with others instead of truly loving them.

Is it possible to experience such love, joy, and freedom that we're transformed from the inside out?

Is it possible to live like the war is over? Is it possible to experience such love, joy, and freedom that we're transformed from the inside out? That's what happened to Lieutenant Onoda. When he was convinced the war was over, his thoughts, his emotions, and his actions were radically changed. For years, he had stolen food from Philippine farmers in the remote region where he was hiding, but after he came out, he returned to establish a scholarship fund for their children. For three decades, he had continued to fight a war that was over. His thoughts had been consumed with loyalty to an emperor who no longer held the reins of power. He had suffered terribly, but nothing would convince him that his assumptions were wrong. It took a person, one he respected, to find him, challenge the lies he had believed for so long, and order him to step into a new life of freedom.

I believe Jesus is stepping into our jungle and calling us to this kind of freedom. Far too many of us have refused to believe the war is over, and we're stuck in a place where nothing we think, say, or do gives us the freedom Jesus has already graciously given us.

Are you ready to come out of the jungle? Listen to Jesus tell you about His grace.

LEGAL AND VITAL

For many Christians, the summary of what God has done for us in Jesus is that "we're saved so we can go to heaven when we die." Thankfully, that's true, but it's incomplete. Jesus' last words on the cross were, "It is finished" (John 19:30). The Greek word is *tetelestai*, which means "paid in full." It means "the work is completed" or "the debt is paid." Jesus was saying that His death is the perfect, complete, legal payment for the sins of mankind. Nothing is missing; nothing else should or could be added. Those who continue to live in the jungle may say they believe in the saving work of Jesus on the cross, but they live like Lieutenant Onoda, still fighting a war for freedom and obeying a command that has long been out of date.

God's grace isn't just a little bit of help for pretty good people; it's rescuing those who are perishing! Many of us don't see ourselves as hopelessly lost apart from Christ, so we don't fully appreciate the love, freedom, and forgiveness He has won for us on the cross. We could look at many different passages that describe the legal aspects of our redemption, but this is one I especially love:

> At one time we too were foolish, disobedient, deceived and enslaved by all kinds of passions and pleasures. We lived in malice and envy, being hated and hating one another. But when the kindness and love of God our Savior appeared, he saved us, not because of righteous things we had done, but because of his mercy. He saved us through the washing of rebirth and renewal by the Holy Spirit, whom he poured out on us generously through Jesus Christ our Savior, so that, having been justified by his grace, we might become heirs having the hope of eternal life. (Titus 3:3-7)

The Bible often uses courtroom language to describe the grace of God. We were the defendants, charged with a long list of sins, chiefly unbelief and idolatry—putting people, possessions, popularity, or prestige ahead of God in our affections. We had no defense. We were guilty, with no hope of leniency, but Jesus stepped in and said, "I'll take the judgment. I'll pay the price. *Tetelestai*—it is finished!" That's what the cross is about.

But the grace of God doesn't end when we initially trust in Jesus. The *legal* aspect of what Christ has already done for us in salvation is coupled with the *vital* element: His grace empowers us to live, really live, by the truth of the Word of God and in the strength of the Spirit of God. Let me return to Paul's letter to Titus to show how this works:

> For the grace of God has appeared that offers salvation to all people. It teaches us to say "No" to ungodliness and worldly passions, and to live self-controlled, upright and godly lives in

this present age, while we wait for the blessed hope—the appearing of the glory of our great God and Savior, Jesus Christ, who gave himself for us to redeem us from all wickedness and to purify for himself a people that are his very own, eager to do what is good. (Titus 2:11-14)

Grace makes a difference every moment of every day . . . but only if we come out of the jungle. Grace not only assures us of God's forgiveness, but it also gives us an eagerness to live the life we were meant to live, a life that is free and full. In the jungle, life is hard. We're on our own, and we're desperate to get the next thing we need to survive. But when we've come out of the jungle into freedom, the Holy Spirit fills us, empowers us, directs us, and uses us to touch the lives of those around us.

Grace not only assures us of God's forgiveness, but it also gives us an eagerness to live the life we were meant to live, a life that is free and full.

We look forward to an incredible future of a physical resurrection in the new heavens and new earth, but the Christian hope isn't only about the future—it's about today . . . this very moment. New Testament scholar N. T. Wright has written, "Jesus embodied in himself the perfect fusion of 'heaven' and 'earth.' In Jesus, therefore, the ancient Jewish hope had come true at last. The point was not for us to 'go to heaven,' but for the life of heaven to arrive on earth. Jesus taught his followers to pray: 'Thy kingdom come on earth as in heaven.'"[3]

The vital aspect of our redemption is nothing less than experiencing a bit of heaven on earth and sharing it with everyone we meet.

GET REAL

It's hard to imagine all the changes Lieutenant Onoda experienced when he obeyed the major's order and came out of the jungle. While he had been stuck in the past, the world had bounded forward. His world of misguided thoughts suddenly had to be challenged and changed, and he had to learn how to have human connections again.

That's a pretty close parallel to my experience when I came out of the jungle of legalism and moralism. Legalism is the belief that following rules makes us acceptable, and many church people (much like the Pharisees in Jesus' day) go far beyond the Ten Commandments in setting rules for others and themselves to follow. Moralism is the belief that being a good person makes us acceptable. It's not so much about obedience to strict rules; it's much more about being nice enough, kind enough, and honest enough to impress God and others. When I stepped out of the jungle, I realized I'd been suffering from PTRSD: post-traumatic religious stress disorder! I preached each week about the saving grace of God, but I lived like grace ended the day I became a Christian, and it was entirely up to me to prove myself to God.

I taught about the love of God, but I often felt unloved . . . and worse, unlovable.

I taught about God's forgiveness, but I often lived under a toxic cloud of shame.

I taught that Jesus was Emmanuel, "God with us," but I often felt He was either distant or displeased with me.

I taught about the freedom we have in Christ, but I felt chained to the sins and errors of the past.

I taught that I was a child of God, but I lived like an orphan—desperately trying to get what I needed and terrified it would be taken away.

PTSD is a mental health disorder common among combat soldiers and those who are the victims or have witnessed violence. Symptoms include severe anxiety, flashbacks, nightmares, and racing thoughts, especially about the "trigger" event. Those who suffer from the disorder are "always on," hyper-alert to any hint of a threat, and often overreact to even the slightest annoyance.[4] My new diagnosis, PTRSD, is the destructive impact of a grace-empty life. I wish I could say that being a Christian for many years is a guarantee against it, but it's not. And I wish I could say being a pastor is the antidote, but it's not. Grace-deprivation can happen to anyone, even those who are the most devoted to God and His work. When Jesus becomes just a model to follow, a benchmark to reach, or perfection to emulate, we've missed His loving, gracious heart. Christianity was never intended to be us trying to imitate Christ, but rather, us participating in His life.

Our commander is coming into the jungle to bring us out. Jesus speaks a revelation of the gospel that assures us that we're deeply loved, completely forgiven, and totally accepted—not based on our flawed performance, but based on Christ's perfect performance. In my book *Limitless*, I described the wonder of God's grace demonstrated at the cross; in this book, I invite "veterans of spiritual warfare" to realize the war is over, and we're free!

Lieutenant Onoda continued to believe the lie that the war wasn't over, so he didn't experience the joy of freedom. His problem wasn't that he wasn't committed enough, that he wasn't disciplined enough, or that he needed to recommit his life to the emperor every day. He was utterly committed, disciplined, and loyal. That's a picture of many Christians I know, including myself for many years—we're deeply committed, thoroughly disciplined, and fiercely loyal. We've heard reports about freedom all our lives, but we haven't really believed it.

You may be able to teach people about the love of God, but are you sure He delights in you? You may be able to explain the truth of God's forgiveness, but do you feel like you have to "be good enough long enough" to make up for your sins? You may tell people that Jesus is near, but secretly, do you feel that He lives in a different zip code? You may read about the freedom Christ gives, but are your thoughts filled with worry and doubt? You hear messages about God being your loving, generous Father, but are you anxious that you won't have enough to meet your needs?

At a crucial point in my life, I was really struggling in my relationship with God. I was a pastor, pouring my heart out every day to the people in our church, but I was running on empty. I had heard all my life that I needed to carry my own cross, but at that moment, I wondered, *If I have to carry my own cross, what was Jesus' cross all about? I must be missing something—something really important. I'm offering people victory and hope I'm not experiencing myself.* That was the turning point. That was the Commander coming to me in the jungle. I began studying what the cross of Jesus actually accomplished for believers . . . and more particularly, for me! I began to experience the love of the Father, the forgiveness that cleanses and sets free, and the surprise of the Spirit living in and through me in every situation to give me supernatural wisdom, love, and strength. Grace became a gift that has kept on giving.

That's my story, and as I've talked to many others—pastors, elders, teachers, faithful believers, and those who have given up on the faith—I've seen their eyes light up as they understand more of God's revelation of grace for every day. Under the load of legalism and moralism, the Christian life is a grind. It's the crushing burden of a pervading sense of poverty, unhealed hurts, and gutting out each day. I have good news: God has much more for us than that! When John described what it means to experience God's grace every day, he wrote this in his first letter: "See what great love the Father has lavished on us, that we should be called children of God! And that is what we are!" (1 John 3:1) I can almost hear him shout!

Are you and I so thrilled to be God's beloved son or daughter that we want to shout? That's not just a dream, and it's not unreachable. It will be a reality if we answer our Commander's call to come out of the jungle.

A REVOLUTION, NOT A REBELLION

A grace revolution isn't a rebellion against church or God. I'm not advocating that you leave your church because you're upset you haven't been taught the message of grace, and I'm not starting a new denomination. When you and I experience God's grace every day, the truth of God's Word becomes even more precious, and the Spirit of God will lead us and empower us in fresh ways to make a difference. I'm not offering a new text of truth; I'm trusting God to take the scales off your eyes so you can see the glorious truth that has been there all along. Many of us are already quite involved in the activities of the church. The everyday experience of grace probably won't change what we do, but it'll certainly change why and how we do it. Rebels want to destroy institutions, but revolutionaries want to restore and rebuild.

The everyday experience of grace probably won't change *what* we do, but it'll certainly change *why* and *how* we do it.

Sometimes people ask me, "Pastor, when are we going to move beyond the gospel?" I tell them, "Never. It's everything we need all the time in all circumstances." Grace is the foundation for all truth about God, ourselves, our relationship with Him, and how we live. Paul explained this fact in his first letter to the Corinthians: "By the grace God has given me, I laid a foundation as a wise builder, and someone else is building on it. But each one should build with care. For no one can lay any foundation other than the one already laid, which is Jesus Christ" (1 Corinthians 3:10-11).

One writer observes that most of us have "hymnal theology"—we focus on the past or the future, and we have little hope to experience the power and love of God in the present. Yes, we need to be grateful for the cross, and yes, someday we'll be with Jesus face to face, but we often have a huge hole in our theology and experience: we have a very limited expectation of God's presence and power *today*. This hole, though, isn't completely empty. We fill it with "oughts" and "shoulds." We hear a message that has twenty-five minutes of grace and five minutes of application, but all we hear is "You'd better do this or that for God to love and bless you!" (So, in many cases, the problem isn't that grace hasn't been taught. It's that we haven't had ears to hear it.) Any belief in conditional acceptance only makes the hole wider and deeper, and after a while, it's really hard to climb out.

The good news . . . the revolutionary news . . . is that God has already given us everything we need to experience His presence and power. In Peter's second letter, he assured us, "Everything that goes into a life of pleasing God has been miraculously given to us by getting to know, personally and intimately, the One who invited us to God. The best invitation we ever received! We were also given absolutely terrific promises to pass on to you—your tickets to participation in the life of God after you turned your back on a world corrupted by lust"

(2 Peter 1:3-4 MSG). Isn't that what you long for—"participation in the life of God"? Of course it is. That's why you picked up this book.

The legal aspects of redemption are in the past tense: Jesus died for us—and actually, *as* us, He rose from the dead, and He ascended to the throne at the Father's right hand—again, for us and *as* us. (I can't wait to explain all of this later in the book!) These are done and complete. The vital part of our salvation is happening now as we experience the wonder of His love, our motives are transformed, our hearts are filled with gratitude, and we begin to live the life He intended for us. The gospel truly gives you your life back.

Christians are called "the bride of Christ." (The men who are reading this may feel offended, but stay with me.) In a marriage, the wedding happens only once. The wife doesn't need to make a commitment to her husband every day. She's already committed. In fact, he would be deeply confused (and probably offended) if she tried to make a new commitment every day. He would tell her, "Relax. Enjoy my love. We're as married as we're ever going to be, and I'm crazy about you!" In the same way, many Christians desperately recommit themselves to God over and over again, scraping their souls to condemn every sin (and anything they might consider sin, whether it is or not), and they always feel substandard . . . less than . . . on the outside looking in. The legal aspect of marriage is what happened on the wedding day; the vital part is the experience the couple enjoys as they develop a deeper love for one another.

Some of us confuse our justification with our sanctification. When we feel that we're doing well spiritually (we're obeying God, we feel close to Him, we're faithful in Bible study and prayer, etc.), we're convinced we're saved. But when our obedience and discipline sag, or when we're struggling in our walks with God, we wonder if we really belong to God after all. This confusion is lethal! The quality of our obedience doesn't determine our salvation. The "order of salvation" is crucial: we believe, so we obey. If we measure our faith by our obedience, we'll never feel secure in God's love because we can never perfectly obey.

The experience of God's grace revolutionizes individuals, families, churches, and communities as people listen instead of talk, care instead of demand, and love instead of blame. If enough of us join this revolution, it might even change the tone of our cultural and political discourse so we seek to understand instead of to intimidate.

A LOOK IN THE MIRROR

None of us has ever been able to look at our own faces, except in a reflection. To be honest, many of us are obsessed with looking in mirrors to check ourselves out. (Or is it just me?) James, the half-brother of Jesus, wrote that it's important to make sure you're looking in the right mirror or the refection will be distorted: "Do not merely listen to the word, and so deceive yourselves. Do what it says. Anyone who listens to the word but does not do what it says is like someone who looks at his face in a mirror and, after looking at himself, goes away and immediately forgets what he looks like. But whoever looks intently into the perfect law that gives freedom, and continues in it—not forgetting what they have heard, but doing it—they will be blessed in what they do" (James 1:22-25).

For many years, I looked into a grace-deprived, performance-driven mirror, and the reflection left me either deeply discouraged because I wasn't doing as well as I should . . . or proud because I was doing better than someone else. Strangely, my version of the Christian life was leaving out something fairly important: Christ! All the burden was on me to do the right thing in the right way with the right motives, and I failed miserably. I wasn't resting in what Jesus had already done for me, and I wasn't trusting in Him to live His life through me by the power of the

Spirit. I thought I had to elevate my level of righteousness to be acceptable—which means I had to punish myself with harsh condemnation whenever I made a mistake. Even though I'd read the Bible cover to cover and taught a lot of it, I still didn't understand what it means to be "in Christ": in His death to experience His forgiveness, in His resurrection to experience a new life, and in His ascension to share His authority as a fellow heir.

The good news is that the legal part of redemption is completely finished, and the vital part is readily available to each of us all the time. Friend, we might as well take what He has given us and really enjoy it. The problem is that we're slow to believe it because our minds are not yet renewed. Paul explained, "So from now on we regard no one from a worldly point of view. Though we once regarded Christ in this way, we do so no longer. Therefore, if anyone is in Christ, the new creation has come: The old has gone, the new is here!" (2 Corinthians 5:16-17)

Our spirits are new creations, but we need to retrain our ability to "regard" Christ and ourselves. What does this mean? It means we previously believed Jesus' role was to help us become better people so we'd be acceptable to God, but now we realize that's not grace at all! We now see our hopelessness apart from Christ and the completeness of His sacrifice for us. The gospel of sheer grace is true, wonderfully true, but we still often feel unlovable, dirty, and distant from Him. That's our challenge: to come out of the jungle and reorient our thinking, our believing, and our acting to our new freedom—to renew our minds according to what is already true of us in Christ.

MY HOPE FOR YOU

Many people and many churches are stuck in a jungle of religious legalism and a theology that is, in effect, oppressive, crushing, abusive, slavish, and driven by performance to please God and impress others. It motivates by guilt and fear, making people believe they always fall short and can never do enough. Now, we can bring people out of the jungle, but bringing them out is only half of the revolution. We have to lead them to a better place. We need to establish people on the foundation of Christ and lead them to fulfill His divine purpose. I believe God is bringing forth a new breed of ministry that's not afraid to preach the gospel—the complete, grace-filled, liberating gospel. Sadly, our pulpits have been flooded with loud messages about politics, morality, rules, self-help programs, psychological manipulation, and rhetoric divorced from the heart of God. But God is raising up:

True apostles to govern in grace,

True prophets to guide in grace,

True evangelists to gather in grace,

True pastors to guard in grace,

True teachers to ground in grace, and

True believers who grow in grace.

God has given gifted people to the church. He has "brought us out" of darkness to "bring us in" to His light. We've been purchased (a revelation of Jesus as our high priest) and purposed (a revelation of Jesus as king). We are at an important juncture in our gospel revolution: what happens now is crucial. It's the difference between dying in the jungle and walking in a place of joy, love, and power . . . and it isn't really a place . . . it's a Person!

Some of you are still in the jungle. You're still fighting a battle that ended long ago. You're still trying to prove yourself by your performance. Hopefully, you'll hear the call of Jesus, realize (finally) that the war is over, and come out.

Some of you are on the edge of the jungle, and you can't decide what to believe. You've read the leaflets, you've heard the college student, and you now hear your Commander, but the life of the jungle is much more familiar than stepping out into the unknown of freedom.

Many of you have answered the call to come out of the jungle, but you're suffering from PTRSD. Your thoughts are haunted by what you've done or haven't done, you still feel like you need to do more and be more to be accepted, and you live with constant anxiety and an undertone of anger. You're free, but you're not enjoying your freedom.

And some have answered Jesus' call to come out, and you're growing in your faith. You're enjoying your freedom, you're fighting the right battles, and you live with joy and gratitude.

For many years, I taught thousands of points, but in much of that time, I missed the main point. The point is Jesus. He is the One who has given us a new status as cherished children of God. He is the One who has paid the price to set us free. He is the One who invites us to bask in His love all day every day. Before we die, there will always be a struggle, but too often, it's the wrong struggle. For a long time, I struggled to be good enough to earn God's approval, but now it's very different: it's the struggle to think right thoughts about God's grace so He can change me from the inside out. The writer to the Hebrews says that we labor to enter God's rest, so our only struggle is to stop struggling because the war is over and He is the victor.

I've been captured by grace, and I hope you are too.

At the end of each chapter, you'll find a declaration and some reflection questions. Don't rush through these. It's not a speed test! Trust God to speak to you as you think and pray, and use the questions to stimulate rich conversations with your spouse, your friends, or your small group.

DECLARATION:

Jesus, You're my gracious Commander, and I hear your call to come out of the jungle.

THINK ABOUT IT:

1. What are some reasons Christians stay in the jungle instead of responding to God's call to come out and enjoy freedom?

2. Explain the differences between the legal and vital aspects of salvation.

3. Have you, or someone close to you, suffered from "Post-traumatic Religious Stress Disorder"? If so, what caused it?

4. What would it mean for you to be part of a "grace revolution"?

5. What do you hope to get out of this book?

CHAPTER 2

THE FATHER'S LOVE

UNLOVABLE VS. ADORED

THE DEEPEST LONGING OF THE HUMAN HEART IS TO BE FULLY known and fully loved. To be known but not loved is terrifying; to be loved but not known is superficial. We thrive only when someone knows the very best and worst about us . . . and loves us still.

Some of us come from horrific backgrounds. We've suffered physical, sexual, verbal, or emotional abuse (or a combination of them), or we've known the emptiness that comes from abandonment. It's human nature to project our perception of our authority figures onto God and assume He's like them. It's no wonder those of us who have endured such pain often have difficulty believing God delights in us!

Others, like me, have enjoyed loving, stable childhoods, but there's something about the human condition that communicates we're not worthy of love. Everything in our culture screams that our acceptance—and our value as human beings—is based solely on our performance, so we're driven to succeed at all costs, or we're driven to please people to win their approval, or we "hide in plain sight" so no one will know the fears that consume our hearts and minds. I'm one of those people. I've never doubted my parents' love, but for many years, I measured myself by the accolades I received (or didn't receive), my appearance, my accomplishments, social media likes, and every other visible yardstick of success.

There's a deeper problem: It's not just that we feel unloved. Many of us also feel unlovable. If I'm unloved, it's your fault, but if I'm unlovable, it shows there's something very wrong with me. We try to fill the gaping hole with anything and everything, and for brief moments, we feel relief. But before long, we're empty and desperate again. We live with a profound illusion that somehow we can do enough and be enough to win the love we crave.

The gospel of grace explodes this illusion, but it's actually bad news before it's good news. It tells us that we were so sinful it took nothing less than the death of the Son of God to pay for our sins, but it assures us that Jesus loves us so much that He was glad to sacrifice himself for us.

The false gospel of Pharisaic religion isn't much different from the secular ladder of success and acceptance—it just uses the Bible to pressure us to perform. The Pharisees demanded that people not only follow the 619 commands in the Bible but also obey the hundreds of extra ones they wrote. Their leverage was fear, with a side order of guilt. They assured people that God stood with His arms crossed and a sneer on His face, watching to see if they make the slightest mistake so He could blast them with condemnation. The twin motives of fear and guilt are very effective . . . but they have devastating consequences. People may obey the rules, but they want to stay far away from the rule-enforcer.

Grace shows us a very different picture: Jesus didn't have His arms crossed and a scowl on His face; His arms were nailed wide open, and His face communicated compassion to the thief hanging next to Him . . . and to us.

Those who are in the jungle (and those who have just come out and are trying to adjust to the new realities) need a transformation of their view of God. He isn't fierce and condemning, He's not distant or completely absent, and He's not looking for ways to blame. On the cross, Jesus prayed, "Father, forgive them, for they do not know what they are doing" (Luke 23:34). Who was He talking about? The hateful, jealous Pharisees whose solution to the threat of His popularity was to have Him killed, the crowd that came to heckle as they watched the show, and the hardhearted Roman soldiers who cared more about gambling for His clothes than His suffering and death. If Jesus could love them so much that He would forgive them, surely we can believe Him when He says He loves us, too! Jesus comes into the jungle to bring us home, and when we're out, He gently reminds us of His love so that our PTRSD gradually subsides and fear is replaced with security.

TURNING THE GREAT COMMANDMENT ON ITS HEAD

I'm going to ruffle some feathers with this point, but it's essential, so here goes. If you ask Christians throughout our country and the world what's the most important biblical principle or rule, the vast majority would refer to a quote from Jesus. One of the experts of the law asked Him, "Teacher, which is the greatest commandment in the Law?"

Jesus replied: "'Love the Lord your God with all your heart and with all your soul and with all your mind.' This is the first and greatest commandment. And the second is like it: 'Love your neighbor as yourself.' All the Law and the Prophets hang on these two commandments" (Matthew 22:36-40).

Who would argue with that? Actually, I would. Let me explain two points: First, commanding someone to love simply doesn't work on its own. If you don't believe me, go home and command your spouse to love you, command your children to love each other, and command people on either side of the political aisle to love each other—it's not going to happen! The teacher asked Jesus "which is the greatest commandment *in the Law*?" The law was given to show us our depravity and emptiness apart from God's grace—yes, including His grace in the Old Testament sacrifices that pointed people to the ultimate sacrifice in Jesus. The law isn't wrong or sinful or irrelevant. Paul explained that it's a necessary "tutor" that shows us the way to Jesus. Yet the law can't save; it only reveals sin. The law can't inflame love; it only condemns.

There's nothing at all wrong with love for God being the highest form of Christian devotion, but we simply can't give what we don't possess.

And second, there's nothing at all wrong with love for God being the highest form of Christian devotion, but we simply can't give what we don't possess. There's a preceding step: we have to experience the love of God before we can love Him in return. Ironically, when we try to love God more, we often feel more empty, confused, and frustrated. We look at the Ten Commandments as the perfect law, and the first of them says, "You shall have no other gods before me" (Exodus 20:3). In other words, knowing God should be our deepest desire and our highest goal, but Moses' instruction didn't start with "the Big Ten." He tells the Israelites in the previous chapter that when we believe in God, we become

His "treasured possession" (Exodus 19:5). God becomes *our* treasure only when we grasp the reality that we're *His* treasure. (For more on this, see the chapter, "Two Treasures," in *Limitless*.) To put it another way, we can't (not just won't, but *can't*) love God with all our heart, soul, mind, and strength until and unless we're overwhelmed with the fact that He loves us with all of His heart, soul, mind, and strength!

When we communicate the requirement of the Great Commandment to love God, we need to quickly add John's clear explanation of how this happens: "We love because he first loved us" (1 John 4:19). He doesn't love us *because* we love Him. His love is unconditional and unlimited. John also explains: "There is no fear in love. But perfect love drives out fear, because fear has to do with punishment. The one who fears is not made perfect in love" (1 John 4:18). Perfect in love. What a thought! A sure sign that we're still in the jungle or that we're still suffering from PTRSD is that in the depths of our hearts, we believe God's love for us is conditioned on our love for Him. We try to love Him, and we may feel close from time to time, but we eventually conclude that we're colossal failures at loving God, and He has every reason to turn His back on us. At least for the sensitive among us, guilt, fear, and shame are oppressive.

When well-meaning church leaders turn the Great Commandment into the mission of the church, we've got it exactly backwards. When the law is our mission, vision, and purpose, we drive people deeper into the jungle. Our attempt to point people to God backfires, and we heap condemnation on them because they simply can't live up to the demands of the law.

As a diagnostic exercise, take a long hard look at two things: your sense of failure in your walk with God, and your prayers. Do you read the command to love God with all your heart and feel terrible about your devotion to Him? Or when you pray, do you say, "God, help me love You more. I really need to do better at this!"[5]

Before the cross, people were under the law, and they had only partial relief from their guilt through their sacrifices. After the cross, we don't read of any commands to love God. Instead, we find scores of passages that remind us of His love for us. Are there commands to obey in the New Testament? Certainly, but always in the context of God's love giving us the motivation to obey with joy. One of my favorite passages that demonstrates the right order of love and obedience is in Paul's letter to the Ephesians: "Get rid of all bitterness, rage and anger, brawling and slander, along with every form of malice. Be kind and compassionate to one another, forgiving each other, just as in Christ God forgave you. Follow God's example, therefore, as dearly loved children and walk in the way of love, just as Christ loved us and gave himself up for us as a fragrant offering and sacrifice to God" (Ephesians 4:31—5:2). Pay attention: Are we to forgive those who offend us? Yes, but we can forgive only to the extent we're gripped with the fact that Christ has forgiven us. Are we to follow God's example? Certainly, but only as we bask in the reality that He has adopted us as His own. Are we to love others? You bet, but our love for them is a direct reflection of how well we've absorbed Jesus' love for us.

Paul was a brilliant theologian and a leader who was as tough as nails, but his encounter with Christ on the Damascus road melted his heart. This demanding, driven man became tenderized by the love of Jesus. Earlier in his letter to the Ephesians, he prays, but it's not your average, everyday prayer. He erupts with a heartfelt plea that God would do a work in the hearts of believers so that we'd be overwhelmed with the love of God:

For this reason I kneel before the Father, from whom every family in heaven and on earth derives its name. I pray that out of his glorious riches he may strengthen you with power through his Spirit in your inner being, so that Christ may dwell in your hearts through faith. And I pray that you, being rooted and established in love, may have power, together with all the Lord's holy people, to grasp how wide and long and high and deep is the love of Christ, and to know this love that surpasses knowledge—that you may be filled to the measure of all the fullness of God.

Now to him who is able to do immeasurably more than all we ask or imagine, according to his power that is at work within us, to him be glory in the church and in Christ Jesus throughout all generations, for ever and ever! Amen. (Ephesians 3:14-21)

What does it take to truly experience the love of God? It requires the power of the Spirit to break down walls of fear and doubt, the tender work of God's compassion in the depths of our souls so we're convinced He adores us, and the revelation that His affection is far, far, far greater than anything we can possibly imagine! It's no coincidence that Paul ends with a benediction about the amazing power of God to convince us that His love is real. And when we get even a taste of it, we'll enjoy more peace, gratitude, and sheer joy than we ever imagined, and we'll want everyone we know to enjoy it, too. That's what the love of God does in us, for us, and through us.

When we put this kind of boundless, soul-satisfying, transforming love next to the conditional and superficial love of the world, we see a stark contrast:

Conditional love requires us to do everything just right, or else . . .

Unconditional love gently guides and redirects.

Conditional love is easily withheld.

Unconditional love is tenacious.

Conditional love is based on feelings, which can easily flip or fade.

Unconditional love is based on a covenant.

Conditional love is really self-focused, not self-giving.

Unconditional love is more interested in giving than getting.

Conditional love keeps a checklist of meeting performance goals.

Unconditional love understands that all of us fail from time to time.

Conditional love uses threats, even subtle ones, to control.

Unconditional love may have limits and boundaries, but always for the other's good.

Conditional love punishes with criticism, blame, or silence.

Unconditional love corrects with kindness and hope.

Conditional love is based on "chemistry."

Unconditional love looks beyond gender, age, personality, race, and nationality.

TOO MUCH STRUGGLE

I believe many of us are either miserable or discouraged in our Christian lives because we've got it all backward. We live under law instead of under grace. (We'll go deeper into that later.) We've been taught that we have to obey or else, that God is angry when we make the smallest mistake, and if we sin, especially "in that way" again, He might just give up on us for good. In the jungle, every day is a grind.

The slogan for Alcoholics Anonymous is "One day at a time." For some of us, our Christian lives are more like "one hour at a time." We've settled into a pattern of toughing out each minute of each day. We may sing the songs on Sunday morning, and we may say "Amen" a time or two during the message, but when we're alone, we feel like something is terribly wrong with us. We're sure: "It just shouldn't be this hard!"

Actually, that's a true statement: it shouldn't be that hard, and it won't be that hard when we're convinced that the love of God is rich and real . . . not just for other people, but for us, too.

When I married Kim, I wandered around for a long time in the bliss of her affection for me. Loving her wasn't a task, it wasn't a struggle, it wasn't something I had to force myself to do. It came naturally because I felt her love so deeply. (I sure hope she would say the same thing about me!)

King David was a busy man. He united the tribes of Israel into a kingdom, fought foreign armies, and administrated justice. He could have been pulled in a thousand directions, but one thing captured his attention:

> One thing I ask from the Lord,
>   this only do I seek:
> that I may dwell in the house of the Lord
>   all the days of my life,
> to gaze on the beauty of the Lord
>   and to seek him in his temple. (Psalm 27:4)

He saw the Lord as beautiful. How do you respond when you see a gorgeous scene in the mountains? What feelings grab your heart when you look at your favorite painting or sculpture? What is beautiful to you? Is the Lord? For many years when I was in the jungle, very little was beautiful to me. I was too busy to stop and look around, and I was too afraid I wouldn't accomplish enough and people would consider me to be a failure. When Jesus came for me in the jungle, I saw His beauty, and the sight changed me. My heart was filled and my motivations redirected. I'm not alone. The former slave trader turned pastor, John Newton, wrote a number of wonderful hymns, including "Amazing Grace." In another of his songs, he described the life-changing power of seeing God for who He really is:

> Our pleasure and our duty,
> Though opposite before;
> Since we have seen his beauty,
> Are joined to part no more.
> To see the law by Christ fulfilled
> And hear His pardoning voice,
> Transforms a slave into a child,
> And duty into choice.[6]

Is your walk with God too much duty and not enough beauty? That's certainly true for many of us. We're wise to let the Spirit of God shine a light into our hearts and show us what's really there. The pain of exposure is quickly erased by the joy of limitless forgiveness and love.

Is your walk with God too much duty and not enough beauty?

MORE THAN WORDS

Years ago, I read a fascinating article that really surprised me. In "Five Ways Jesus Revealed Grace," Paul Ellis observed that in the four Gospels, we don't find Jesus mentioning the word "grace," not even once.[7] The law, though, appears many times, but we don't need to worry that Jesus somehow missed the point. His entire life was a demonstration of God's amazing grace. His incarnation, humility, and sacrifice for ungrateful people are the epitome of unmerited favor for the undeserving. He didn't need to use the word *grace* to communicate the message. Grace is Jesus . . . Jesus is grace.

A similar point is that Jesus never said, "I love you" to an individual. When I think about particular scenes in the Gospels, I see love exemplified over and over again. Perhaps the most poignant to me is in the opening scenes in Mark:

> And a leper came to Jesus, beseeching Him and falling on his knees before Him, and saying, "If You are willing, You can make me clean"
>
> Moved with compassion, Jesus stretched out His hand and touched him, and said to him, "I am willing; be cleansed."
>
> Immediately the leprosy left him and he was cleansed. (Mark 1:40-42 NASB)

What a demonstration of selfless love! Lepers were considered the lowest of the low, the least of the least. They were shunned and relegated to "colonies" where they were out of sight and where contagion would be held in check. This man undoubtedly had heard that Jesus could do miracles, so he came out of the colony and begged Jesus to heal him. The Pharisees would have run away and shouted condemnations at him for his insolence, but Jesus reached out and touched the man's rotten flesh, and he was instantly healed. Someday, in the replay room in heaven, I want to see this scene. I want to see the looks on the faces of Jesus, the leper, and the other people watching.

Another clear depiction of Jesus' love was in His first sermon. After He had been tempted in the desert, He returned to Nazareth and went to the synagogue. The day's reading was providential. He opened the scroll of Isaiah and read:

> "The Spirit of the Lord is on me,
>> because he has anointed me
>> to proclaim good news to the poor.
> He has sent me to proclaim freedom for the prisoners
>> and recovery of sight for the blind,
> to set the oppressed free,
>> to proclaim the year of the Lord's favor."

He rolled up the scroll, sat down, and told the crowd, "Today this scripture is fulfilled in your hearing" (Luke 4:16-21). And this Scripture applies to all of us: All of us were bankrupt in spirit, all of us were prisoners of sin, all of us were blind to the truth, and all of us were in chains, bound to the dark forces of the spiritual world. But Jesus proclaimed "the year of the Lord's favor," the year of Jubilee when all debts are cancelled, slaves are freed, and land reverts to the original owners—a picture of grace if there ever was one![8]

When we read this passage, we understandably stop when Jesus stopped reading. It appears that He was defining His mission, and in fact, He was . . . but there was more to His mission than the proclamation of blessing. The rest of the last verse in the Scripture from Isaiah says, "To proclaim the year of the Lord's favor, and the vengeance of our God." The part He read was what He came to give away; the part He didn't read is the part He could only take on himself—becoming our substitute by absorbing the vengeance we deserve. Both are evidences of His overflowing grace to us.

NOW, REALLY?

Some people who are reading this chapter are thinking, *Brother, aren't you forgetting something? God's anger is displayed over and over in the Bible, and He hates sin!*

Please don't misunderstand. I'm not teaching universalism that someday God will accept everybody no matter who they are or what they've done. Judgment is one of the most common themes in the Bible. How should we understand all the references to God's anger and wrath? Thankfully, the Bible is crystal clear: it's all about the cross. When Jesus died, was it a demonstration of God's justice to punish sin, or was it the greatest display of His love the world has ever seen? Yes and yes! In two sentences in his letter to the Romans, Paul put these two together: "God presented Christ as a sacrifice of atonement, through the shedding of his blood—to be received by faith. He did this to demonstrate his righteousness . . . at the present time, so as to be just and the one who justifies those who have faith in Jesus" (Romans 3:25-26). When Jesus breathed His last with the words, "It is finished," the penalty for sin was completely, totally paid. There would never need to be another sacrifice for sin. Justice was fulfilled. Jesus paid it all. Why did He do it? To make us right with Him (justified) so we could enjoy unfettered love, kindness, compassion, purpose, and strength. Justice and love were both present in the cross of Jesus.

We don't obey God to be forgiven and made right with Him; instead, we obey Him out of sheer gratitude because we've already been forgiven and made right with Him!

We don't obey God to be forgiven and made right with Him; instead, we obey Him out of sheer gratitude because we've already been forgiven and made right with Him! If our standing with God is earned, it's no longer grace. Paul explained, "Now to the one who works, wages are not credited as a gift but as an obligation. However, to the one who does not work but trusts God who justifies the ungodly, their faith is credited as righteousness" (Romans 4:4-5). Our entrance into a new status as chosen, adopted, forgiven children of the King is based on our admission that we deserve condemnation, not acceptance. Far too many of us still don't get it. We read the Bible and sing the hymns, but we still try to do enough (working to earn God's love) instead of trusting that when we believed in Him, a radical change happened in our status and our hearts.

Now, the only way God looks at us, treats us, and responds to us is in love. How does a loving mom treat a child who is trying to please her but makes a mess? She's thrilled with the child's heart and overlooks the cake batter on the floor. How does a loving dad treat a child who lied? Not with a fierce blast of rage, but by holding him close, assuring him of forgiveness, and talking about why honesty is important. Do these parenting scenarios seem wrong to you as I relate them to God? If they do, you haven't yet grasped the wonder of grace.

One of the enemy's most effective lies is that no matter how much we read the Bible, pray, serve, and give, we're still on shaky ground with God, and we have to continually prove ourselves to Him. Somewhere in the depths of our hearts, we secretly wonder if God could really love us, so we keep looking to our performance to win His affection. In one way, this is a perfectly normal response. Everything in our culture is based on performance—everything but the unconditional love of God. Even the very best parents are still affected to some degree by the self-validation throughout our culture. They may be wonderfully loving and consistent, and their love is a huge head start for their kids, but God's love is infinitely deeper and sweeter.

Don't we need to do something to win God's love? Can all this really be true? Yes, it's true, and yes, it's yours right now. Ask the Spirit of God to open the eyes of your heart to see what you already have in Christ. You don't need to earn a status of a beloved child—you already have it!

As much as anyone, I know what it's like to struggle to believe the magnificent truth of God's unconditional love. In the past few years, in my own life and as I've talked to countless people about God's grace, I keep coming back to the moment at the Jordan River when Jesus went to John the Baptist to be baptized. Matthew's Gospel takes us there: "As soon as Jesus was baptized, he went up out of the water. At that moment heaven was opened, and he saw the Spirit of God descending like a dove and alighting on him. And a voice from heaven said, 'This is my Son, whom I love; with him I am well pleased'" (Matthew 3:16-17). This affirmation of the Father's love came before Jesus preached a single sermon, told a single parable, healed a single person, or performed a single miracle. The Father's voice and the Spirit's presence confirmed what He already knew: The Father was pleased to call Him His beloved Son completely apart from any performance.

Some might push back, "Yes, but that's Jesus, and I'm certainly not Him!" Oh, don't miss this. When we believe in Christ, we're "in Him." That means that we are identified with Him, as we've seen, in His death, resurrection, and ascension, and it means we're identified with Him at this moment at the river. God is saying to you and me, "You are my son, you are my daughter, whom I love; with you I'm well pleased." Can you take that message into your heart? Will you ask God to make His delight in you more real than ever before?

When Jesus came out of the water and received the validation of the Father and the Spirit, He was immediately led into the wilderness to be tempted (Matthew 4:1-11). What were the enemy's temptations? Three times he questioned the very truths Jesus had just heard: "If you are the Son of God" (v. 3) . . . "If you are the Son of God" (v. 6) . . . "if you will bow down and worship me" (v. 9) . . . I'll give you the kingdoms of the world. Satan tempted Jesus to find love, power, and purpose in something or someone other than the Father . . . but Jesus said, "No thanks."

As we expose our minds and hearts to the glorious truth of God's amazing love, we'll be tempted, too. The enemy will whisper (or shout) that God's affirmation isn't really true, we still have to earn His love, and what God offers isn't quite enough to satisfy us. Those were the temptations in the Garden of Eden and in the desert, and they're the same today. Be ready for them. When we're sure of our status as God's children, we won't be afraid of temptation, and we'll resist it far better. Each time, it's just another opportunity to confirm who we are as God's dear son or daughter. We already have all we need; we have all we could ever want.

Jesus resisted Satan's offers because He was convinced the Father's love gave Him absolute security and stability. He had nothing to prove and nothing to lose. It's the same for you and me. When we're convinced that we're the beloved sons and daughters of the King, we'll have the wisdom and strength to resist the lie that we still have to prove ourselves to earn God's approval. We'll be more thankful, more joyful, more loving, and more eager to honor the One who loves us so much.

About three years after Jesus' baptism and temptation, we find Him on a mountain with Moses and Elijah, along with Peter, James, and John. It wouldn't be long until Jesus would go to Jerusalem to die, and again, the Father speaks to Jesus, but even more, to the three disciples:

"This is my Son, whom I love; with him I am well pleased. Listen to him!" (Matthew 17:5)

I believe God is saying the same thing to you and me.

Have you heard the voice of the Father? Are you listening?

DECLARATION

Father, I'm listening.
Speak Your words of love to my heart.

CONSIDER THIS:

1. Do you agree or disagree with the premise of this chapter that many Christians believe they still need to earn God's love? What are some evidences?

2. What are some reasons it's essential to get the order of love right: to experience God's love as the source of our love for Him?

3. Is the Lord beautiful to you? Be honest. How can you tell?

4. Which of the pairings of conditional and unconditional love do you struggle with? How might the truths in this chapter help you believe in God's limitless love?

5. What are some messages (from family, church, friends, school, business, etc.) that powerfully communicate that love is conditional? How can you resist them?

6. What happens when we truly listen to God's words of affirmation?

CHAPTER 3

NEVER GOOD ENOUGH?

LAW VS. GRACE

I HAD FINISHED A WORSHIP SERVICE, AND I WAS GREETING people as they left the church. As person after person stopped to shake my hand and greet me, I noticed a man standing near the window. He didn't look like he was leaving, but he wasn't making any moves toward me. The look on his face told me he really needed some help. He waited until the last person had walked away, and finally, he approached me. "Pastor," he began though his eyes were still looking down, "I'm not too sure about what you said today."

"What part of it?" I asked. "I'd be happy to talk more about it."

"The, uh, the part about God's forgiveness."

"Tell me what you're having trouble with."

He looked at me with a pained expression and blurted out, "You can't tell me that God has forgiven me! Not really. Not me."

"Oh," I tried to assure him, "Christ's sacrifice paid for all our sins."

I couldn't tell if he was going to cry or throw up. He told me, "But . . . but you don't know what I've done. I've done some . . . really bad things. I'm sure God forgives other people, but I just can't believe God would forgive me."

I wish I could say this was an isolated instance, but it's not. Many people live under a cloud of doubt about God's forgiveness. Some have done something so horrendous that it's unimaginable that God could forgive them, and others have done something wrong so many times that they feel outside the reach of God.

The solution for many people is a Protestant form of penance. They don't recite prayers or get instructions from a priest; instead, they have self-imposed punishment to feel bad enough long enough. By the end of that time, they hope they've done enough for God to forgive them. It doesn't take a theologian to recognize this is another "work" people do to earn favor with God. It's not grace, it's not forgiveness, and it's not the way of the cross.

It seems that many people think of forgiveness as a nice thing God does for pretty good people, kind of a wink and a nod that "everything is going to be okay, so don't worry about it." But they know what they've done deserves more than that. Instinctively, they know their selfishness has created a debt, and someone has to pay it. The self-punishment of penance is their way of paying it themselves, and they assume that's the best they can hope for.

They're wrong . . . dead wrong. The price has already been paid, and it's plenty to cover the debt of any and every sin—and then some. It's enough if it's a "little white lie" that got them out of trouble at home, in school, or at work, and it's still enough for those who have committed the most heinous crimes. In fact, some of those who have fallen the furthest have the clearest grasp of the wonder of God's forgiveness. Some of the most humble, grateful, kind people I've ever met are men on death row who have fallen to the very bottom and found Christ there. They're still paying society for their sin, but Jesus has taken the burden of spiritual alienation and eternal condemnation on himself in their place . . . and they know it. Even when they made their bed in a kind of living hell, they found Him there.

Paul uses a strange word to explain the extent of God's forgiveness. We actually looked at it earlier in a different translation. He described the effect of the cross: "[all who believe] are justified by his grace as a gift, through the redemption that is in Christ Jesus, whom God put forward as a propitiation by his blood, to be received by faith" (Romans 3:24-25 ESV). We don't use the word *propitiation* very often, but it's packed with theological meaning. It means "to satisfy justice and take away wrath that is deserved" or "the sacrifice that satisfies completely." When we were outside of the family of God, we deserved God's righteous justice, but Jesus took the punishment we deserved so we could have the honor and love He deserves. That's quite a swap!

That's quite a swap!

CONFESSION AND REPENTANCE

Some people object, "But Ben, doesn't the Bible say we have to confess or we're not forgiven? And doesn't it say we have to repent to be forgiven?" No, if we put any requirement of what we have to do in order to be forgiven, it's law, not grace.

These people look at the first chapter of John's first letter, and they're sure confession is the prerequisite to forgiveness. It reads: "If we confess our sins, he is faithful and just and will forgive us our sins and purify us from all unrighteousness" (1 John 1:9). They say, "See! It says it right there: "If we confess, God will forgive." But they missed the part in the middle. God is faithful to forgive because He has already paid the price. It's done. It's over. It's complete. To confess means "to agree." In this case, it means we agree with God that what we've done is selfish and wrong, and we agree with Him that Christ's sacrifice is sufficient to pay for it. Confession isn't the necessary trigger to *get* forgiven; Christ has *already* paid that price.

Far too often, we don't want to confess because we don't believe we're already forgiven. Instead of feeling the warmth of God's cleansing love, we minimize, "It wasn't that bad," we excuse, "It wasn't my fault," we blame, "It's his fault," or we deny, "It didn't even happen." We'll do anything to avoid feeling exposed to condemnation! This goes back to the view of God with His arms crossed and a scowl on His face. We think He's saying, "Yeah, tell Me about it, and I'll make sure you hurt enough that you'll never think of doing that again!" But that's not God's heart at all. He holds His arms wide open and says, "Come to Me. You can be honest with Me because there's no fear that I'll blast you into next week. In fact, when you confess your sins to Me, it will be a covenant renewal ceremony, and you'll be more aware of how close I've always been!"

Okay, one down, but what about repentance? Isn't it necessary for forgiveness? After His death, burial, and resurrection, Jesus appeared to various individuals and groups. Near the end of Luke's Gospel, He again appeared to the disciples. To prove that He wasn't a ghost, He ate some fish. He took this opportunity to explain again why He came: "Then he opened their minds so they could understand the Scriptures. He told them, 'This is what is written: The Messiah will suffer and rise from the dead on the third day, and repentance for the forgiveness of sins will be preached in his name to all nations, beginning at Jerusalem'"

(Luke 24:45-47). Notice that it says, "*and* repentance for the forgiveness of sins will be preached." In *The Gospel in Ten Words*, Paul Ellis uncovers the difference between "for" and "and":

> Now take a moment to go and check that passage in your own Bible. What does it say? Does it say "repentance *for* forgiveness" or "repentance *and* forgiveness"? The difference is huge. Repentance for forgiveness is what John the Baptist preached. It's forgiveness conditional on you turning from sin. It's a verb for a verb.
>
> But this is not what Jesus is saying here. He doesn't use verbs for repentance and forgiveness but nouns. He's saying, "From now on, forgiveness is not something God *does*, it's something he's *done*."[9]

COMPLETE FORGIVENESS

Christ's sacrifice is *sufficient* for all—He died "for the sins of the world"—but it is *efficient* only for those who believe. My faith in "complete forgiveness" doesn't mean I believe every person will go to heaven. It means that the offer is universal, and Christ's sacrifice eradicates the sins of those who put their trust in Him—their past sins, no matter how heinous they may be; their present sins, no matter how shameful they are; and their future sins, whatever selfish acts they commit from now on. Some object: "Future sins? Are you kidding?" No, I'm not kidding. When Jesus died, all of your sins were future, even the ones you don't know about yet.

Others protest, "Doesn't that just give people a license to sin?" Yes and no. It assures people that forgiveness isn't granted in a miserly way, and it isn't given only as a reward for the right kind of confession or a certain depth of emotion. So, yes, it provides enormous freedom. But if we have any inkling of the love underneath God's forgiveness, we won't take advantage of our freedom. In fact, as beloved children of the King, we'll want to honor Him in everything we think, say, and do. A rich understanding of forgiveness, then, doesn't lead to more sin—it leads to a life of ever-deepening devotion inspired by the wonder of God's love. Paul encouraged the wayward believers in Galatia: "You, my brothers and sisters, were called to be free. But do not use your freedom to indulge the flesh; rather, serve one another humbly in love" (Galatians 5:13). That's his answer to the question of whether complete forgiveness gives a license to sin.

> **A rich understanding of forgiveness, then, doesn't lead to more sin—it leads to a life of ever-deepening devotion inspired by the wonder of God's love.**

Sometimes people ask me, "Pastor Ben, are you saying that I can do anything I want because I'm already forgiven?" That's the wrong question. People do whatever they want anyway. The right question is, "Why do you want to do what you do? What are your motives?" Why would anyone want to go back to the pigpen and eat the slop of sin when Jesus has given you a place at His banquet table?

FORGIVING YOURSELF

As any family counselor knows, withholding love and forgiveness is a powerful way to manipulate people. In a desert of affection, they become desperate for any sign of affirmation, or even a single kind word.

This desperation makes them do anything to please, they feel driven to prove they're worthy of love, or they give up and hide to avoid being hurt again.

I believe many of us use the same techniques on ourselves. When we punish ourselves by calling ourselves horrible names, and we withhold pleasures as a form of self-punishment, we're trying to control our future choices. Self-pity feels so right. We grovel in our self-condemnation, and we're certain we deserve even more. *Surely*, we tell ourselves, *if I feel this bad about myself, I must really be a good person, right?*

Wrong. I can't tell you how many times people have said, "Pastor Ben, I know God has forgiven me, but I just can't forgive myself." For many years, I said things like, "Oh, poor thing. Let me explain it again." But the problem isn't a lack of knowledge; it's pride. Yes, pride. Self-hatred is believing our view of life, God, and ourselves instead of believing God's view. Self-condemnation becomes a way of life. It's also called shame. And many of us stay there our entire lives! Being "unable to forgive ourselves" is really unwillingness to believe what God says about the depth of His forgiveness.

Shame and guilt are related, but there's a significant difference. Guilt says, "I did something bad"; shame says, "I'm bad." Popular author and psychologist Brené Brown writes:

Based on my research and the research of other shame researchers, I believe that there is a profound difference between shame and guilt. I believe that guilt is adaptive and helpful – it's holding something we've done or failed to do up against our values and feeling psychological discomfort. I define shame as the intensely painful feeling or experience of believing that we are flawed and therefore unworthy of love and belonging – something we've experienced, done, or failed to do makes us unworthy of connection. I don't believe shame is helpful or productive.[10]

Those who refuse to accept God's forgiveness don't make the distinction between feeling remorse, which reminds us of God's forgiveness, and crushing shame that leaves us feeling empty, alone, and helpless. In the mind of a person racked with shame, every flaw, every sin, and every mistake is a catastrophe: "See, I must be a terrible person to think that, say that, or do that!" We become our own accuser, judge, and executioner.

Tragically, many people in the church believe religion is the solution to their shame. They want some kind of structure, a list of rules, some expectations they can meet to feel better about themselves, and most churches are only too happy to provide these. But they're grace killers. If we do these things to earn God's forgiveness, we're back under the law. Don't get me wrong. If a genuine grasp of God's forgiveness overflows from our hearts, we'll want to read the Bible, but to know more about the God who adores us, not to cut some notches on our spiritual holsters; we'll want to pray, but to connect with the heart of God, not to earn points; and we'll give and serve, but to share the love and forgiveness we've received, not to climb an imaginary ladder of acceptability.

MEDS

Shame is an oppressive monster. We can't live with it very long before we look for ways to distract ourselves and numb the pain. Of course, we instantly think of alcohol and drugs as medications people turn to, but we can easily broaden the category to include distractions that numb us, like too much time watching television, video games, sleeping too much, incessant noise to drown out thought, living with clutter, working extra hours, refusal or inability to make decisions, and overeating. We can also include distractions that excite, like pornography, shopping, multitasking, and social media. The list of "medications" we use to distract or numb us is unending.

A friend of mine is a church leader who made an appointment with a counselor to ask for help with chronic anxiety. As they talked, the counselor asked him how he spent his time. My friend listed a lot of activities. The counselor then asked, "How often are you still and quiet?"

My friend was surprised by the question. He laughed nervously and said, "Well, never."

The counselor observed, "I don't think you feel comfortable with yourself, so you always fill the time with something so you don't have to think and feel very deeply."

Busyness was my friend's med. "Um, so, what do I do about that?" he asked.

The counselor replied, "It's not a matter of time management. It's all about heart management. You need to experience much more love, and you need to heal the hurts you've suffered so you don't feel driven to avoid your feelings."

I now see the church as a rehab center, a place where people come to get off the addiction of empty religion. My job is to provide an environment where every aspect of self-righteousness is challenged and the gospel of grace is taught and lived every day. Like me for so many years, most people naturally resist grace. We'd rather earn something than receive a gift. Only needy people receive gifts, and we don't want to be perceived as needy! But we were. In fact, we were desperately, unutterably needy. That's what makes it so wondrous that Jesus stepped out of the glory of heaven to live and die in our place. Grace is hard to grasp because it goes against everything in human nature and our culture. I love Martin Luther's advice to pastors: "Most necessary it is, therefore, that we should know this article [of the gospel of grace] well, teach it unto others, and beat it into their heads continually."[11]

COVERED OR FORGIVEN?

In the Old Testament, we often read that God has "covered" sin. When something is covered, like with a blanket, it's out of view, but it's still there. The animal sacrifices covered the sin of the person making the offering, but they didn't take it away. The writer to the Hebrews draws the distinction between the Old and the New:

> The law is only a shadow of the good things that are coming— not the realities themselves. For this reason it can never, by the same sacrifices repeated endlessly year after year, make perfect those who draw near to worship. Otherwise, would they not have stopped being offered? For the worshipers would have been cleansed once for all, and would no longer have felt guilty for their sins. But those sacrifices are an annual reminder of sins. It is impossible for the blood of bulls and goats to take away sins. . . .
>
> But when [Jesus] had offered for all time one sacrifice for sins, he sat down at the right hand of God, and since that time he waits for his enemies to be made his footstool. For by one sacrifice he has made perfect forever those who are being made holy. (Hebrews 10:1-4, 12-14)

Does this distinction really matter? Yes, it matters a lot! Some of us act like we're Old Testament believers, glad that a momentary lapse can be covered up by going to church, giving a little more, or not cussing for a whole day. But this is a long way from the reality of a New Testament, gospel-drenched, Christ-bought complete forgiveness that assures, cleanses, and restores. God doesn't dab forgiveness on our sins. It's not partial, and it's not momentary. All of our sins—the ones that haunt us and the ones we don't even notice because we're blind to them—were put on Jesus when He hung on the cross. The blood of bulls and goats only covered sin, but it was still there. The blood of Jesus obliterates sin and sets us free to enjoy His love and forgiveness.

The Old Testament, though, wasn't barren of the promise of grace. The sacrifices, the tabernacle and the temple, and the prophets pointed to something—actually Someone—far better than what they experienced. God gave Jeremiah a glimpse of a new covenant, a covenant of grace:

"The days are coming," declares the Lord,
     "when I will make a new covenant
with the people of Israel
     and with the people of Judah.
It will not be like the covenant
     I made with their ancestors
when I took them by the hand
     to lead them out of Egypt,
because they broke my covenant,
     though I was a husband to them,"
declares the Lord.
"This is the covenant I will make with the people of Israel
     after that time," declares the Lord.
"I will put my law in their minds
     and write it on their hearts.
I will be their God,
     and they will be my people.

No longer will they teach their neighbor,
    or say to one another, 'Know the Lord,'
because they will all know me,
    from the least of them to the greatest,"
declares the Lord.
"For I will forgive their wickedness
    and will remember their sins no more."
    (Jeremiah 31:31-34)

There are two brands of forgiveness: one comes from Mt. Sinai and Moses' teaching in the wilderness, and it's partial; the other comes from Mt. Calvary, and it's complete. Many of us treat God's forgiveness like a *debit* card. We have to put something in so we can draw on it to cover each sin (or at least the ones we're aware of), but it's more like a limitless *gift* card, one that draws on the treasure house of heaven! The psalmist exclaimed, "Happy are those whose sins are forgiven, whose wrongs are pardoned. Happy is the one whom the Lord does not accuse of doing wrong and who is free from all deceit" (Psalm 32:1-2 GNT). Does the thought of God's forgiveness make you happy? Relieved? Thrilled? Amazed? If it doesn't, it's probably not the real thing you're thinking about.

BEYOND TOLERATING

For years, my best thoughts about God were that He tolerated me. Most of us have enough friends that our circle includes at least one person we tolerate. We'd rather they not join the party, and if they do, we hope they stay in another room. When we see them coming, we hope they're going to walk past us. When they stop to talk, we hope it's over pretty quickly. Do you know what I'm talking about? That's how I

thought God saw me: the friend He could only tolerate but He really
didn't like very much.

For years, my best thoughts about God were that He tolerated me.

In His most famous story, Jesus paints a very different picture of
the Father. Let me describe the context: Jesus was hanging around with
people who were decidedly outside the mainstream of Jewish society.
Luke calls them "tax collectors and sinners." The men who collected
taxes were considered traitors because they were collecting money for
the occupying Roman army. And the designation of "sinners" was used
for a broad category of prostitutes, pimps, thieves, and other unsavory
characters. I can picture Jesus enjoying being with them . . . and then,
up walked the religious elite, the Pharisees and teachers of the law. They
couldn't stand the people Jesus was with, and they muttered, probably
in a stage whisper so everyone could hear, "This man welcomes sinners
and eats with them" (Luke 15:2). In this scene, you could cut the tension with a knife!

Jesus used this teachable moment to tell three stories that all had
one message. A shepherd had a hundred sheep, but one of them got
lost. He went out into the country to find it and bring it back. He was
thrilled and threw a party! A woman had ten coins and lost one of them
on the dirt floor of her home. When she found it, she was so excited that
she threw a party to celebrate!

In the third story, a man had two sons. The younger one insulted
his father by asking for his share of the estate . . . something that happened only after a parent had died. He was saying, "Dad, I wish you

were dead!" His part was a third of the estate. His father sold off land and livestock, gave the money to his selfish son, and watched him walk out of his life. The young man threw it all away on wine, women, and song, and he found himself in the despicable position of feeding pigs—and thinking the slop looked delicious! He "came to his senses" and realized the hired men on his father's estate lived a lot better than he did, so he started walking home. He didn't expect to be welcomed. He only wanted to be a laborer so he could pay his father back.

You know the story: "But while he was still a long way off, his father saw him and was filled with compassion for him; he ran to his son, threw his arms around him and kissed him" (v. 20). How would you have expected the father to respond when he saw his son? I might think he would put his hands on his hips and sneer, "So, you've spent it all and come back for more. Well, that's all you're going to get!" Or "What are you doing here? If you're going to apologize, it better be good!" But that's not at all how the father treated his son. In fact, he didn't even let him finish his prepared confession. "But the father said to his servants, 'Quick! Bring the best robe and put it on him. Put a ring on his finger and sandals on his feet. Bring the fattened calf and kill it. Let's have a feast and celebrate. For this son of mine was dead and is alive again; he was lost and is found.' So they began to celebrate" (vv. 22-24). The robe replaced the filthy rags he was wearing, the ring gave him the power to conduct contracts for the family, the sandals gave him comfort for his tired and calloused feet, and the party . . . the party showed the unmitigated joy of the father that his son had returned!

Was this toleration? No way! This is a picture of God's radical, shameless, unbounded love for us—so spectacular that forgiveness was granted without even being requested. In fact, we can conclude that the entire time the younger son was "in a far country" wasting his inheritance and dishonoring his dad, the father had already forgiven him.

That's the reason he was looking down the road anticipating the silhouette of his son in the distance. Forgiveness wasn't given grudgingly; it was showered on the young man. In this way, we see that forgiveness and love are inextricably linked in the heart of God . . . and present in our experience as we begin to fathom the depths of His affection.

But there's more to the story. The older son was working in the fields. When he heard the sound of the party, he asked what was going on. When he learned that his little brother had come home and his father was throwing lavish celebration, he was furious and refused to join in! His father graciously went out to the field to personally invite him, but he still refused. The story ends with a picture of two responses to forgiveness. The younger son didn't expect to be forgiven and fully accepted back in the family, but that's the measure of his father's love. The older son showed his true colors when he barked at his dad, "Look! All these years I've been slaving for you and never disobeyed your orders. Yet you never gave me even a young goat so I could celebrate with my friends. But when this son of yours who has squandered your property with prostitutes comes home, you kill the fattened calf for him!" (vv. 29-30)

You may be very familiar with this parable, but let me push on it a little and connect it to the complete forgiveness God gladly grants. The story is usually called "the prodigal son," but it should be plural, "the prodigal sons," because neither son knew the heart of their father. The younger son obviously missed his heart because we see him selfishly take his inheritance and blow it. The older son never left the house, but he was lost in his self-righteousness. In other words, just because someone is in the house doesn't mean he is captured by the Father's heart.

The younger son was well aware of his sins, but his father's love and forgiveness were much greater. The older son had obeyed and worked very hard, but in all those years, he didn't experience his father's tender, kind, loving heart. Jesus wants us to put ourselves in the story: Are you and I like the younger son, who turned to the Father because we had done things so selfish that we had nowhere else to go—and we saw Him bounding to us, hugging us, kissing us, and fully welcoming us back? Or are you and I more like the older son, trusting in our obedience and hard work for the Father but missing His heart? The younger brother came back in shame, but he was welcomed as a son. The older brother had been a son, but he thought of himself as a slave . . . and he missed the party.

Remember the opening scene of this story. Who was Jesus speaking to? The younger brother represents the tax collectors and sinners the Pharisees detested. But the real audience was the group of Pharisees and teachers of the law. Jesus was asking them, "Can you see yourself in the older son? When you look in the mirror, do you see an obedient but self-righteous and angry person who is far from the Father's heart? That's what I see when I look at you. Like the father in the story, I'm inviting you to come to the feast of love and forgiveness. I'm inviting you to turn from the idolatry of self-effort and experience the kindness of God that transforms hearts. Will you come?"

In the first two stories about the lost sheep and the lost coin, someone went to look for what was lost. In the third story, though, no one goes out. We may not notice this detail, but the people sitting around Jesus would have realized it at once. Who should have gone into the far country to bring the wayward son home? It was the older brother's role, but he didn't have enough love to prompt him to go. And how would the younger brother be fully restored to the family after he had wasted his inheritance? Full sonship would come only at the expense of the older brother. He would need to give his brother a third of what was left, and he didn't want to do that. In our lives, who came to the far country to find us and bring us back? Jesus. He left heaven and came to earth to find us. What was the cost to Him? Not just a third of His inheritance, but His very life. He gave everything to bring us home to the Father. He is the true elder brother.

When I teach and preach about the glorious, sweeping forgiveness of God, some people think they're helping me when they say, "Remember, Pastor, we're not forgiven unless we repent."

I open the Bible to this passage in Luke and point to it. I say, "The father forgave before the young man ever showed up, and he wouldn't even let him finish his confession. We try to make forgiveness conditional, but it's unconditional. Even the fact that the younger son 'came to his senses' is a work of the Spirit of God to awaken us to our need to be forgiven. The entire message of forgiveness, then, is much more about the kindness of God than a checklist we have to follow."

The younger son in Jesus' story came out of the jungle to enjoy his father's forgiveness and delight, but the older son didn't even realize he was in the jungle of self-righteousness and self-pity. The Father in our story is calling all of us to come out of the jungle.

DECLARATION:

Father, thank You for the boundless,
joyful forgiveness You've showered on me.

THINK ABOUT IT:

1. What are some forms of "Protestant penance"? Why do they seem so attractive?

2. What are some ways you've seen people "medicate" the pain of feeling unloved, unwanted, and unforgiven? What do these meds promise? What do they deliver? Which, if any, of these have you used?

3. Why is it important for us to realize our sins are completely for-given instead of being temporarily and partially covered?

4. Put yourself in the story about the father and his two sons. How would you have felt if you were the younger son and you saw your dad running toward you? What would those minutes have been like when he interrupted your confession and fully restored you to the family?

5. Do you think there are many Christians who are like the older son in the story? Explain your answer. What's so attractive about this perspective? How is it spiritually deadening?

CHAPTER 4

SLOW SUICIDE

STILL STRIVING VS. IT'S FINISHED

IN THE MIDDLE OF PAUL'S LETTER TO THE COLOSSIANS, HE writes some things that many of us overlook because they're out of the realm of how we normally think: "Since, then, you have been raised with Christ, set your hearts on things above, where Christ is, seated at the right hand of God. Set your minds on things above, not on earthly things. For you died, and your life is now hidden with Christ in God. When Christ, who is your life, appears, then you also will appear with him in glory" (Colossians 3:1-4). Wait a minute! Do I look like I've been raised with Christ and seated with Him on the throne at the right hand of God? And what does Paul mean "you died"? I'm reading this, aren't I? So I can't be dead. How is my life "hidden with Christ in God"? Okay, the last part is something I understand. There will be a day when I'm resurrected and enjoy face-to-face connection with Jesus in the new heavens and new earth . . . but Paul seems to be connecting that to the rest of what he writes in this passage—and he's saying it has already happened and is true right now. What's going on here?

When you ask a hundred Christians what happened on the cross, virtually every one would say, "Jesus died for our sins." That's true, but that's not the whole story. Paul is telling us that something else happened: you and I died, too. If we're "in Him," then what happened to Him applies to us. The effectiveness of His sacrifice was credited to us: His death is the substitute for the death we deserved.

When we look more closely at Paul's letters, we see this teaching over and over. For instance:

- In Galatians, he wrote, "I have been crucified with Christ and I no longer live, but Christ lives in me. The life I now live in the body, I live by faith in the Son of God, who loved me and gave himself for me" (Galatians 2:20).

- He reminded the Corinthians, "For Christ's love compels us, because we are convinced that one died for all, and therefore all died. And he died for all, that those who live should no longer live for themselves but for him who died for them and was raised again" (2 Corinthians 5:14-15).

- In a letter to his protégé Timothy, Paul included an early hymn that began: "Here is a trustworthy saying: If we died with him, we will also live with him" (2 Timothy 2:11).

- He explained to the Romans that the only way to experience the life of Christ is to participate in His death: "What shall we say, then? Shall we go on sinning so that grace may increase? By no means! We are those who have died to sin; how can we live in it any longer? Or don't you know that all of us who were baptized into Christ Jesus were baptized into his death? We were therefore buried with him through baptism into death in order that, just as Christ was raised from the dead through the glory of the Father, we too may live a new life" (Romans 6:1-4).

As I thought more about these passages, a question resonated in my heart: When I think of the cross and imagine being there, where am I in the story? Am I in the crowd? Am I one of the faithful women or John who watched and wept? Or am I on the cross in Jesus? Paul's answer is clear: I'm on the cross as Jesus died the death I should have died, and three days later, I'm coming out of the tomb in the newness of life with Him. I co-died with Him, and I was co-resurrected with Him.

That's what Paul meant when he called us "a new creation." At the moment we trust in Christ to be our Savior and Lord, we aren't the same person we used to be. There has been a funeral and a resurrection.

SLAVE OR FREE

Before the Civil War, very few slaves were freed by their masters, and a few others found a way to buy their freedom, but for the vast majority, there was only one escape from the oppressive world they endured: death. In his great letter to the Christians in Rome, Paul continues his explanation of this important truth, and he takes it from the abstract to the practical. First, he makes the connection again between Christ's death and ours:

Now if we died with Christ, we believe that we will also live with him. For we know that since Christ was raised from the dead, he cannot die again; death no longer has mastery over him. The death he died, he died to sin once for all; but the life he lives, he lives to God. (Romans 6:8-10)

Then Paul shows how this reality makes a tremendous impact on how we live each day:

> In the same way, count yourselves dead to sin but alive to God in Christ Jesus. Therefore do not let sin reign in your mortal body so that you obey its evil desires. Do not offer any part of yourself to sin as an instrument of wickedness, but rather offer yourselves to God as those who have been brought from death to life; and offer every part of yourself to him as an instrument of righteousness. For sin shall no longer be your master, because you are not under the law, but under grace. (vv. 11-14)

Do you see the connection? If we aren't sure we've died, we can't really live!

Now, this brings up some obvious questions. What exactly does it mean that "we died"? It's obviously not our bodies that died; it's our old life, our unregenerate selves that were devoted to pleasure, power, control, and approval. When we say "yes" to Christ, we're saying "no" to the idols we've had on the throne of our lives. We're saying, "Those have no power over me any longer. I've found something—actually Someone—far more attractive, far more powerful, and far more life-giving than those counterfeits of meaning. They promised, but they can't deliver. I'm through with them. Those things no longer have power over me. I've died to them."

This biblical concept is reflected in some cultures in the Middle East. If two people have come to a point of irreconcilable differences, they may say to each other, "You're dead to me!" The statement is a declaration that the relationship is over, it's severed, and there's no hope for the future. In the same way, Paul is teaching that our old life is dead to us. We're finished with it, and it has no power over us any longer.

In the same way, Paul is teaching that our old life is dead to us. We're finished with it, and it has no power over us any longer.

And what does it mean that we've been raised with Christ? It means that His heart, His compassion, His purposes, and His vitality are imputed into us. How does this relate to our acts of sin? Every moment of every day, we can choose to live in the truth that we're dead and resurrected in Christ, and as a result experience freedom and the Spirit's power. Or we can ignore that truth (or forget about it), and live like a slave to our desires for things other than God. In *Men Made New,* author and theologian John Stott described the impact of this passage:

> For us, then, it is like this. We deserved to die for our sin. By union with Jesus Christ we did die—not in our own person (that would have meant eternal death) but in the Person of Christ our Substitute, with whom we have been made one by faith and baptism. And, by union with the same Christ, we have risen again to live the life of a justified sinner, a life that is altogether new. The old life is finished. We have died to it. The penalty is borne. We emerge from this death justified. The law cannot touch us, because the penalty is paid.[12]

For many of us, including me for many years, the Christian life is painful and difficult. Oh, we talk about victory and blessing, but we fight with conflicting desires all day every day. Paul's solution is to come to grips with the reality that the fight is over because we're already dead. The slave has been set free!

For a long time, I taught the passages about "dying to self" and concepts of "putting yourself on the altar." All of these statements sound good and noble and right, but they completely miss the point: we've already been put on the altar, and the sacrifice has already been slain! We're in Christ in His death. We no longer have to beat ourselves up with condemnation to prove we're committed to God, starving ourselves of joy, and enduring a slow spiritual and emotional suicide. Ironically, the secret of really living is to be convinced that we're already dead!

PRACTICE, PRACTICE

Two of the most common sacraments of the church display the truth that we've died and been made alive in Christ. When a person goes under the water in baptism, it's a symbol of burial—only dead people get buried! Then, when the person comes up out of the water, it's a symbol of new life in Christ.

When we participate in the Lord's Supper, the cup represents the cup of judgment Jesus drank when He bore our sins on the cross, and the bread reminds us that Jesus is "the Bread of Life" who nourishes our hearts with His kindness, compassion, wisdom, and strength. Matthew puts us at the scene:

> While they were eating, Jesus took bread, and when he had given thanks, he broke it and gave it to his disciples, saying, "Take and eat; this is my body."
>
> Then he took a cup, and when he had given thanks, he gave it to them, saying, "Drink from it, all of you. This is my blood of the covenant, which is poured out for many for the forgiveness of sins. I tell you, I will not drink from this fruit of

the vine from now on until that day when I drink it new with you in my Father's kingdom." (Matthew 26:26-29)

The next time you watch a baptism or participate in Communion, think: *That's me, too. I'm dead in Christ, and I'm alive in Him. Thank you, Jesus, for this revolution in me!* It'll keep you from drifting off and thinking about lunch.

TODAY AND EVERY DAY

I think most of us struggle at the wrong level of consciousness. We have this thought or that desire, and we try to figure out if it's the right one or not. We're tempted, and we justify our decision based on any number of factors, but after we've made the decision, we're filled with self-doubt. Instead, we need to go several layers down and contemplate the deeper realities: We're slaves of something, it's inevitable, but will we be slaves of sin or slaves of God? Where does our allegiance lie? Paul explained:

What then? Shall we sin because we are not under the law but under grace? By no means! Don't you know that when you offer yourselves to someone as obedient slaves, you are slaves of the one you obey—whether you are slaves to sin, which leads to death, or to obedience, which leads to righteousness? But thanks be to God that, though you used to be slaves to sin, you have come to obey from your heart the pattern of teaching that has now claimed your allegiance. You have been set free from sin and have become slaves to righteousness. (Romans 6:15-18)

This teaching from Paul gets us back where we started: "Set your minds on things above, not on earthly things." Paul paints a sharp contrast between two lives: the old life and the new—the one that was devoted to sin and would have led to eternal death and destruction, and the new one that connects us with the heart and mind of God and results in spiritual growth and eternal life. The Christian life isn't endless drudgery of trying to reform who we used to be. That's the "human potential movement" and "Dr. Phil" philosophy. The "things above" are the gospel truths that tell us not only what happened to Jesus when He was on the cross, but what happened to us: we died with Christ so that we could be raised to new life in Him. This life isn't drudgery . . . it's the adventure we were created to enjoy!

The choice between the two lives, though, isn't always an easy one.

The choice between the two lives, though, isn't always an easy one. The pull of the world and the lies of the enemy are strong, so we need to keep digging deeper into the truth of our identity in Christ to fight well. In this last passage, Paul repeated an attack by his adversaries: "Shall we [continue to] sin because we are not under law but under grace?" They accused him of using grace to encourage sinful behavior. His response was emphatic: "By no means!" or in another translation: "God forbid!" It takes that kind of fierce commitment to remain slaves of the right Master.

One powerful illustration of the biblical truth that we're dead in Christ is found in the series, *Band of Brothers*. The episodes track Easy Company of the 101st Airborne Division from training in North

Georgia, to the D-Day landings, through France and Belgium, and into Germany through the end of World War II. They were in some of the most dramatic battles of the European war. One of the platoon leaders, Lieutenant Ronald Spiers, amazed everyone with his incredible bravery. It was clear there was nothing that he was hesitant to do. He had played a major part on D-Day in the capture and destruction of the German artillery at Brécourt Manor that had been pounding the soldiers landing on the beaches. Later, one night near the French village of Carentan, Private Albert Blithe confessed to Spiers that he had been a coward and had hidden during the fighting on that first day of the landing. "You don't see how simple it is," Spiers told him.

Blithe was confused. "Simple, sir?"

"Just do what you have to do," the lieutenant told him.

Blithe almost cried as he said, "I was afraid."

Spiers looked into his eyes and told him, "The only hope you have is to accept the fact that you're already dead. The sooner you accept that, the sooner you'll be able to function as a soldier is supposed to function. . . . All war depends upon it."[13]

Suddenly, Blithe (and those of us who watch the episode) understand the source of Spiers' courage: he considered himself already dead, so nothing threatened him, and he had nothing left to lose.

I believe this is the message of Scripture for us: Too many of us are afraid of losing something we don't really possess. If we consider ourselves already dead in Christ and alive in Him, we'll live with incredible courage, selflessness, and joy.

RENEWING THE MIND

We're bombarded with messages every day. The cumulative effect is powerful. A journal of psychology reports that the average American is subject to between four and five thousand advertisements a day, and sixty-two percent of shoppers buy products just to cheer themselves up. It's a form of self-help we call "retail therapy."[14] Add to that total the messages communicated by our spouse, kids, parents, teachers, boss, friends, and neighbors. And then there's the news. Our nation has become so polarized that many of us have concluded that people who disagree with us aren't just wrong, they're evil! We speak about each other, and often to each other, in the most spiteful, un-Christlike ways, and we feel empowered by our anger. (I hope I'm not talking about you, but you certainly know people like this.)

My point is that we're standing against hurricane-force winds of opinions, pleas, and manipulation, and we enjoy only a few breezes of affirmation and encouragement. We're new people, with a fantastic new status and a new identity, but we still live in a messy world. The voices that compete with God's truth are loud and constant: these voices come from the world, the flesh, and the enemy of our souls. We often think of them as separate enemies, but they're closely interconnected. The *world* is the opposition to God and His kingdom in the broad context of culture and society. The *flesh* isn't our physical bodies but our natural inclination to be selfish—our old, unrenewed mind. And the *enemy* is an angelic being who rebelled against God, led other angels to follow him, and uses temptation, deception, and accusation to overcome God's truth in the minds of believers and unbelievers. In practice, here's how it works: we live in a smog of confusion about God and we experience opposition to Him, our inclination is to believe the lies and reject the truth, and Satan uses the messages coming from the world and our wrong thoughts to steer us off course from God's best.

The battle is in the mind. How we think determines what we believe, and what we believe shapes our actions. The Bible is filled with admonitions to "consider," "think," "set your mind," "let no one deceive you," and "ponder." Our task is to do the hard work of recognizing lies and replacing them with truth, and we're soldiers in this fight. Paul explained to the Christians in Corinth:

> For though we live in the world, we do not wage war as the world does. The weapons we fight with are not the weapons of the world. On the contrary, they have divine power to demolish strongholds. We demolish arguments and every pretension that sets itself up against the knowledge of God, and we take captive every thought to make it obedient to Christ. (2 Corinthians 10:3-5)

What are the "arguments and pretensions"? They're thoughts that lean hard against the gospel of grace. They tell us that God doesn't care, He isn't in control over all things, and He's very unhappy with us. They insist that the way forward is to try harder to be a good person, to be more disciplined, more committed, and more zealous for God. They blame us for not feeling passionate enough, not loving God enough, and not doing enough for God. They're effective in the lives of believers because they use the Bible, and they often come out of the mouths of Christians.

What are the weapons we fight with? The truths of the gospel of grace. It's not enough to be religious, and in fact, religion alone is a deadly poison. The gospel corrects our perspective of God, of ourselves, and of how we grow in our faith. Grace is, to put it mildly, countercultural. In fact, I hate to say it, but the message in many churches is mostly religion. The preachers and teachers talk about Jesus dying for our sins, but they don't communicate how the grace of God changes everything. Our identity is radically changed the moment we trust in Christ, but our minds need constant renewal so they focus on the things above and build up defenses against the world, the flesh, and the enemy.

Let me illustrate what renewing the mind looks like. When someone wants to become a plumber, he starts with only a desire but with very little knowledge. If he didn't learn the trade, he'd flood basements, break disposals, and hook up the wrong pipes all over a customer's house. He knows that to become a master plumber, he needs time as an apprentice under someone who has the skills to impart. At first, he makes some mistakes, but the master plumber oversees him and doesn't let him get too far out of hand. Gradually, the apprentice gains knowledge, and he sees how to put that knowledge into practice. At some point, what he has learned becomes second nature—he doesn't even have to think about the things he was so confused about at the beginning. They come naturally.

In his book, *After You Believe*, N. T. Wright cites the story of the aborted airline flight of US Airways 1549 from LaGuardia Airport in New York to Charlotte, North Carolina. On takeoff, the plane hit a flock of geese, and both engines lost power. Instantly, Captain Sullenberger had to decide how to save the passengers. Two local airports were nearby, but either path would risk crashing into populated areas, and the plane was too far away to turn back to LaGuardia. He quickly thought through his options and concluded that his best choice was to put the plane down in the Hudson River. He and his copilot went through dozens (or maybe hundreds) of steps to prepare the plane and the passengers for a water landing. As they approached the water, Sullenberger turned the plane to go with the flow of the river, turned off the engines, and pulled the nose up so the plane could land flat instead of digging into the water. The next scenes were of ferries and other boats rushing to the plane to take the passengers off the wings. No one was hurt. People said it was a miracle!

Wright disagrees. He says that a life that is in tune with the gospel of grace, a life full of, in his terms, "virtue," doesn't just happen. For years, Captain Sullenberger had flown in many different situations, and his choices that day above New York were the product of his training.

Years of study and experience had given him a "renewed mind." Wright explains:

> Virtue is what happens when someone has made a thousand small choices requiring effort and concentration to do something which is good and right, but which doesn't come naturally. And then, on the thousand and first time, when it really matters, they find that they do what's required automatically. Virtue is what happens when wise and courageous choices become second nature.[15]

Attending church is a good thing. Reading the Bible is also a good thing. So are prayer and giving and serving. But an hour or so a week does little to combat the powerful onslaught of lies and half-truths we're subjected to every day. And even doing these things isn't productive if our assumptions are that doing more religious activities is the answer to every spiritual problem. We need to see the drastic contrasts: light and darkness, virtue and selfishness, humility and pride—and see the negative factors in our hearts so we'll say, "God forbid!" and feast our minds on the marvelous truths of the gospel of Jesus.

Wright says that acquiring the truth, training, and skills of living a gospel-shaped life is much like learning to play a musical instrument or a sport. At first, every effort feels unnatural, and we make many mistakes. But with practice, especially under a gifted teacher, we gradually learn to play better and better. At some point, the finger placement on the instrument or the athletic stance that seemed so awkward at first becomes normal ... so normal we don't even have to think about it. This isn't "works" instead of "grace." We don't earn any points with God by going through this learning process. Quite the opposite: it's the pursuit of grace with all our hearts.

The truth that we died with Christ when He was on the cross adds another dimension to our understanding of the upside-down kingdom:

the way up is down, the way to have power is to serve, the way to honor is humility, the last shall be first and the first last, and the way to experience real life is to recognize we've already died in Him. These concepts are affronts to our cultural hopes and expectations, but this is the way of the cross . . . this is the way of Jesus.

DECLARATION:

For I died, and my life is now hidden with
Christ in God.

THINK ABOUT IT:

1. What difference does it make to see yourself on the cross with Jesus instead of being in the crowd?

2. When we trust in Christ, we're effectively saying to our old life, "You're dead to me." What does that mean in practical terms for you?

3. Does it offend you or liberate you to think of yourself as formerly a slave of sin who has now become God's slave? Explain your answer.

4. What are the categories of messages that come to you each day? Think of the sources, the volumes, and the power of them. How would you describe the impact of these messages?

5. How well are you fighting against the "arguments and pretensions" that bombard you?

6. What has it taken (or more likely, what will it take) for the truths of the gospel of grace to become second nature to you? Are you willing to make this happen? Why or why not?

CHAPTER 5

BELONGING

DISTANT VS. CLOSE

FOR ME, LIVING IN THE JUNGLE MADE ME FEEL DIRTY AND DISTANT, not forgiven and adored. The longing of our hearts is to know that we're loved . . . without strings attached . . . to be wanted, to be cherished. When we read the Bible, it doesn't take long to realize the stark contrast between how people felt about God in the Old Testament and how they felt about Jesus in the New Testament. We could look at many passages, but the following ones illustrate the point.

After God miraculously freed His people from slavery in Egypt and parted the sea for them to escape Pharaoh's army, He led them to Mt. Sinai. He instructed Moses to climb the mountain to meet with Him, but He ordered the people to stay away:

"Put limits for the people around the mountain and tell them,
'Be careful that you do not approach the mountain or touch
the foot of it. Whoever touches the mountain is to be put to

death. They are to be stoned or shot with arrows; not a hand is to be laid on them. No person or animal shall be permitted to live.' Only when the ram's horn sounds a long blast may they approach the mountain." . . .

On the morning of the third day there was thunder and lightning, with a thick cloud over the mountain, and a very loud trumpet blast. Everyone in the camp trembled. Then Moses led the people out of the camp to meet with God, and they stood at the foot of the mountain. Mount Sinai was covered with smoke, because the Lord descended on it in fire. The smoke billowed up from it like smoke from a furnace, and the whole mountain trembled violently. As the sound of the trumpet grew louder and louder, Moses spoke and the voice of God answered him. (Exodus 19:12-13, 16-19)

The presence of God terrified them! "When the people saw the thunder and lightning and heard the trumpet and saw the mountain in smoke, they trembled with fear" (Exodus 20:18). As you remember, God led the people by day with a moving pillar of cloud and by night with a pillar of fire. They constructed a tabernacle in the wilderness, and later they built the temple in Jerusalem. The historian tells us that when King Solomon dedicated the temple, something happened that overwhelmed everyone there:

When Solomon finished praying, fire came down from heaven and consumed the burnt offering and the sacrifices, and the glory of the Lord filled the temple. The priests could not enter the temple of the Lord because the glory of the Lord filled it. When all the Israelites saw the fire coming down and the glory of the Lord above the temple, they knelt on the pavement with

their faces to the ground, and they worshiped and gave thanks
to the Lord, saying,

"He is good;

his love endures forever." (2 Chronicles 7:1-3)

The Holy of Holies, the place in the temple where God dwelled, could be entered by the high priest only once a year on the day of atonement (Yom Kippur) to offer sacrifices. The presence of God was both terrifying and overwhelming to the people. God commanded the people to keep their distance, but it was never God's heart to exclude anyone.

But in the New Testament, we see something completely different. Jesus touched lepers, the blind, and the sick. He became friends with the high and the low, the elite and the outcasts. He wasn't feared, but He was despised by the ruling class because He was "a friend of sinners." We see the compassion of Jesus in scene after scene. For instance, when Peter saw Jesus walking on the water on a stormy night, he asked if he could join Him. Jesus invited him out of the boat, but Peter became afraid and began to sink. "Immediately Jesus reached out his hand and caught him. 'You of little faith,' he said, 'why did you doubt?'" (Matthew 14:31)

Other people steered clear of those who were demon-possessed, but Jesus' tender love compelled Him to move toward them. People near the Sea of Galilee were afraid of the naked man who lived in the tombs and broke every chain used to control him. Mark tells us, "Night and day among the tombs and in the hills he would cry out and cut himself with stones" (Mark 5:5). Jesus engaged the man (and the demons), cast the demons out, and clothed the man. In an obvious Christological statement, Mark records Jesus' instructions and the man's response: "'Go home to your own people and tell them how much the Lord has done for you, and how he has had mercy on you.' So the man went away and began to tell in the Decapolis how much Jesus had done for him. And all the people were amazed" (vs. 19-20). Mark is telling us that Jesus, the one who relates with tender, strong love, is the God who inspired terror at Sinai.

But if we understand that in Jesus our connection with God has been radically changed, we can rest in His abundant grace.

If we only believe in the God of Sinai, we may conclude that we can never do enough to please Him, and we're stuck in the performance trap. But if we understand that in Jesus our connection with God has been radically changed, we can rest in His abundant grace. Trying to prove ourselves—to God and to people—is exhausting, but Jesus invites us, "Come to me, all you who are weary and burdened, and I will give you rest. Take my yoke upon you and learn from me, for I am gentle and humble in heart, and you will find rest for your souls. For my yoke is easy and my burden is light" (Matthew 11:28-30).

CLOSER

We often think we need to "get closer to God," and we go through all kinds of spiritual gymnastics to try to accomplish this. How do we know if we're trying hard enough? Quite often, we measure our dedication by the intensity of our emotions: passion, tears, joy, and grief. There's certainly nothing wrong with having emotions, but far too often, we get the cart before the horse and believe the intensity of our heartfelt passion proves our devotion to God, instead of basking in God's covenant devotion to us and letting the emotions flow from that relationship.

When we realize the truth that we're "in Christ," our conception of the relationship changes. How can we get any closer than being dead in Him and alive in Him? How can we get any closer than being seated with Him at the right hand of the Father? How can we get any closer than Him living in us? As we saw in the last chapter, Paul explained to the Roman Christians that we're united with Jesus in His death and resurrection. When Paul wrote his first letter to the Corinthians, he had to challenge their thinking about sin and righteousness. They were arguing with each other about food, sex, and relationships of all kinds. He told them bluntly:

> The body, however, is not meant for sexual immorality but for the Lord, and the Lord for the body. By his power God raised the Lord from the dead, and he will raise us also. Do you not know that your bodies are members of Christ himself? Shall I then take the members of Christ and unite them with a prostitute? Never! Do you not know that he who unites himself with a prostitute is one with her in body? For it is said, "The two will become one flesh." But whoever is united with the Lord is one with him in spirit. (1 Corinthians 6:13-17)

How do we get closer to God? Most of us think, "If I study the Bible just a little longer each day, if I pray a little more, if I have more powerful emotions when I think of God, if I . . ." We believe it's entirely up to us to do something (anything!) to feel closer to God. But we have the wrong measuring stick. Our feelings are fickle, and for some of us, they lead us down the wrong road pretty quickly. It's easy to assume the level of our passion isn't high enough, so we need to do more to rev up our emotional engines. We look around in church and marvel at those who are singing with tears running down their faces and people who are on the floor crying out to God. Again, there's nothing wrong with these responses . . . as long as they're genuine. Yet when we compare ourselves to the people who are most emotionally expressive, we're using the wrong measuring stick.

But what if we came to the conclusion that we're already as close to God as we can possibly get, and He has taken the initiative to draw us to himself? He has moved into us. He's made us His home address! He's the true older brother who came from the splendor of heaven to the pigpen of earth to find us and bring us home. He's the One who lavishes His love on us—not because we've earned it but only because He cherishes us.

He's made us His home address!

Our union with Jesus is safe and sure. It was bought with His blood, assured by His resurrection, and authenticated by His ascension to the right hand of the Father.

Before I understood this concept (and remember, I was a pastor!), I longed to feel closer to God. My solution was to read one more book, attend one more conference, try to pray with a little more emotion, and beg God to be closer to me. There were, to be sure, some spikes in my emotions and I sometimes felt close to Him, but far more often, I left those activities groveling in guilt because I was sure I couldn't do enough to win God's affection. I faced one of two conclusions: either something was terribly wrong with God, or there was something terribly wrong with me. Neither option was reassuring! I couldn't come to the place that I thought God was flawed, so the only right answer was B—I was so backward, so deeply messed up, that I couldn't be close to God no matter how hard I tried and no matter how much I pleaded. It's no wonder I was frustrated and discouraged!

That's why this revelation of my union with Christ has been so revolutionary. I no longer carry the burden of trying so hard to feel closer to God. I'm there. I'm in Him, in His heart and in His thoughts all day every day. For years I used Old Testament terror and requirements of performance to try to measure up. How well did that work for the people who came out of Egypt? Not too well, and it didn't work any better for me. In the new covenant, the totality of God's love, forgiveness, and acceptance is settled, not because I've prayed so hard, felt so passionate, or done so much to earn it, but only by sheer grace. What a relief! What difference does it make? Stay tuned . . .

HIS LIFE, MY LIFE

Christianity is Christ. I can't say it any plainer than that. He didn't come to give us a self-improvement program. He came to identify so much with us that when He died, we died; when He rose, we rose. Earlier, we looked at Colossians 3:3: "For you died, and your life is now hidden with Christ in God." In the next verse, Paul closes the loop: "When Christ, who is your life, appears, then you also will appear with him in glory." Yes, someday Jesus will come back, and we'll be with Him in glory, but don't focus only on the future. Paul insists that Christ is our life today, right now, this minute.

The Christians in Galatia began well but went way off track. After Paul left, some Jewish teachers came from Jerusalem and taught that the believers still had to follow the law to be right with God. When Paul heard about it, he fired off a letter to correct their thinking. He was so upset it was like his hair was on fire! He explained in no uncertain terms that the law was incapable of saving them. The law, as we've seen, has a very useful purpose: to show us our need for grace. Paul told them how it works:

> For through the law I died to the law so that I might live for God. I have been crucified with Christ and I no longer live, but Christ lives in me. The life I now live in the body, I live by faith in the Son of God, who loved me and gave himself for me. I do not set aside the grace of God, for if righteousness could be gained through the law, Christ died for nothing! (Galatians 2:19-21)

For many years, my spiritual life was a grind. It became a joy when I realized it's not even mine to live! Who did I think could do a better job of living the Christian life, Jesus or me? For all that time, I'd been squeezing the branch, pressuring it to produce fruit. When I finally quit trying so hard and started resting in this revelation, the sap began to flow, and I've enjoyed more love and power than I ever imagined possible. Later in the same letter, Paul again contrasted life in the flesh and life in the Spirit, and his point was crystal clear. First, he outlined what it means to live in the flesh:

> So I say, walk by the Spirit, and you will not gratify the desires of the flesh. For the flesh desires what is contrary to the Spirit, and the Spirit what is contrary to the flesh. They are in conflict with each other, so that you are not to do whatever you want. But if you are led by the Spirit, you are not under the law.

The acts of the flesh are obvious: sexual immorality, impurity and debauchery; idolatry and witchcraft; hatred, discord, jealousy, fits of rage, selfish ambition, dissensions, factions and envy; drunkenness, orgies, and the like. I warn you, as I did before, that those who live like this will not inherit the kingdom of God. (Galatians 5:16-21)

Yes, it's a fight between the flesh and the Spirit. The victory comes, not in trying harder and harder, but in finally giving up our trying and choosing instead to trust in God's grace. And the result?

But the fruit of the Spirit is love, joy, peace, forbearance, kindness, goodness, faithfulness, gentleness and self-control. Against such things there is no law. Those who belong to Christ Jesus have crucified the flesh with its passions and desires. Since we live by the Spirit, let us keep in step with the Spirit. (vv. 22-25)

You've read these verses many times, I'm sure, but read them again for the first time with a new insight. Paul contrasts "the acts of the flesh," or in other translations, "the works of the flesh," and "the fruit of the Spirit." We perform works, but fruit is produced in us by the Holy Spirit. And there's no law against it! That means we don't have to worry about whether it's from God. There's no law in the Bible against love, joy, peace, or any of the other aspects of this spiritual fruit. They're produced in us gradually, slowly, and inevitably as we simply rest in the vine. That's the life of Jesus in us.

In His great prayer before He was arrested, Jesus asked the Father to make our relationship with Him just like His relationship with the Father. We have a hard time thinking about the Trinity because we don't understand how three can be one, but that truth is similar to our relationship with God—we don't fully understand how we can be in complete unity with God! Jesus prayed:

> "I have given them the glory that you gave me, that they may be one as we are one—I in them and you in me—so that they may be brought to complete unity. Then the world will know that you sent me and have loved them even as you have loved me." (John 17:22-23)

He prayed this prayer only hours before He went to the cross, and it was answered when He died there. At that moment, the law was fulfilled, death was conquered, and new life was made available to all who believe—and when we trust in Christ, we become one with God.

How dramatic was that moment in Jerusalem almost two thousand years ago? In one of the most amazing scenes in the Gospels, Matthew shows us: "At that moment the curtain of the temple was torn in two from top to bottom. The earth shook, the rocks split and the tombs broke open. The bodies of many holy people who had died were raised to life. They came out of the tombs after Jesus' resurrection and went into the holy city and appeared to many people" (Matthew 27:51-53). What? The priests in the temple must have been stunned when the veil separating people from the presence of God was ripped, with no human hands, from top to bottom. The presence of God became a new reality for those who believe. But that's not all. In one of the most shocking events of that day, the earth shook and dead people rose from their graves—and casually walked around the city! Whatever else that means, it certainly tells us that the sacrifice of Jesus brought new life to dead people . . . people like us who have died with Him and are raised with Him.

MORE THAN A GOOD IDEA

Closeness to God is a gift of grace. It was given to all of us who believe at the moment of our salvation. Fruit grows, but His presence doesn't. The veil has been ripped apart; we live in union with God; it's settled and done. Human relationships are categorically different. In a friendship or a marriage, closeness grows (or fades) over time, but with God, we already have the entirety of His presence. It can never grow, and it can never fade. Certainly, our experience of His closeness is variable, but that's often because we don't yet grasp the wonder of the truth that we're already in Him and He's in us.

It takes the work of the Spirit of God to illumine the Scriptures and use messages and friends to confirm the Spirit's whisper or shout about God's limitless love for us.

The depth of God's grace can't be absorbed only by reading a book, hearing a sermon, or talking to a friend about Jesus. It takes the work of the Spirit of God to illumine the Scriptures and use messages and friends to confirm the Spirit's whisper or shout about God's limitless love for us. We need the Spirit to open our eyes and our ears so we can get it. Paul explained:

> We do, however, speak a message of wisdom among the mature, but not the wisdom of this age or of the rulers of this age, who are coming to nothing. No, we declare God's wisdom, a mystery that has been hidden and that God destined for our

glory before time began. None of the rulers of this age understood it, for if they had, they would not have crucified the Lord
of glory. However, as it is written:

"What no eye has seen,

what no ear has heard,

and what no human mind has conceived"—

the things God has prepared for those who love him—
these are the things God has revealed to us by his Spirit.
(1 Corinthians 2:6-10)

And to the Christians in Rome, Paul taught that the Spirit doesn't
just set us free from the condemnation of the law; He assures us that
we have an intimate, strong connection with the heart of God. He has
adopted us as His own:

The Spirit you received does not make you slaves, so that
you live in fear again; rather, the Spirit you received brought
about your adoption to sonship. And by him we cry, "Abba,
Father." The Spirit himself testifies with our spirit that we are
God's children. Now if we are children, then we are heirs—
heirs of God and co-heirs with Christ, if indeed we share in
his sufferings in order that we may also share in his glory.
(Romans 8:15-17)

"Abba" is significant here. Paul's not talking about the Swedish rock
band from the 70s. This is a primal utterance, like "Dada" or "Mama,"
which assures us that we belong to God in the same way a well-loved
child relates to his or her parents. In that stage of development, a child
learns to trust, to give and receive affection, and feel safe in the presence

of the parents. That's the message God communicates to us as "the Spirit himself testifies" as He whispers to our hearts.

Many of us act like we're in the process of adoption, but it hasn't happened yet. We're sure we need to impress the prospective new parent so He'll love us and accept us. And we act like we're engaged to Jesus, but we're not His bride yet. (Stay with me, men!) But we're "the bride of Christ," not His fiancée. Many of us spend our lives trying to measure up to God's standards, and when we're honest, we know we've failed miserably. But instead of turning to grace, we double down and try even harder. Surely we can do better! Surely we can do more! We live like we're in the wilderness between Egypt and Canaan instead of being in the Upper Room at Pentecost.

When the Spirit opens our eyes, we'll see our union with God throughout the New Testament. For instance, in the opening verses of Paul's circular letter addressed to the Ephesians, he writes:

Praise be to the God and Father of our Lord Jesus Christ, who has blessed us in the heavenly realms with every spiritual blessing in Christ. For he chose us in him before the creation of the world to be holy and blameless in his sight. In love he predestined us for adoption to sonship through Jesus Christ, in accordance with his pleasure and will—to the praise of his glorious grace, which he has freely given us in the One he loves. (Ephesians 1:3-6)

We may not be much in the eyes of some people, but "in his sight," we're chosen, loved, and adopted. And it's not according to our performance, but in accordance with "his pleasure and will"—He's thrilled to have us! We grow in our faith as we increasingly see ourselves, others, and situations the way God sees us. Are you and I "holy and blameless"?

That's how God sees us because we're in Christ, and that's how He sees Jesus. Embrace it, wallow in it, and be thrilled by it. It's true!

The law brings curses and death, but grace brings newness of life. John tried to distill it down to its most fundamental level near the end of his first letter: "And this is the testimony: God has given us eternal life, and this life is in his Son. Whoever has the Son has life; whoever does not have the Son of God does not have life" (1 John 5:11-12). If you have the Son, you have life . . . eternal life. A concept that has a meaning that's far more than a length of time, it signifies a different *quality* of life based on a different *source* of life. We actually know the God who spun the galaxies into being, who stooped to come to us to call us to himself, and who continues to convince us that being "in Him" is more wonderful than we can possibly know.

Does this seem too good to be true? Do you reject (or ignore) this teaching because you can't imagine God's grace being so wonderful, so sweeping, so tender? Ask the Spirit of God to open the eyes of your heart to see this truth. It'll revolutionize your life.

COME FORTH!

When Jesus stood at the tomb of His friend Lazarus, He wept because He knew death wasn't what God intended for us. In the middle of the grieving sisters and the wailing mourners, He called, "Lazarus, come out!" (John 11:43) The dead man came out, but he was still wrapped in the linen strips used for burial. He was alive but still bound by the trappings of death. Jesus told the people standing there, "Take off the grave clothes and let him go" (v. 44). That's my role in the lives of believers. Jesus has made them alive, but they're still bound in their grave clothes they can't experience their freedom. The strips of linen are performance, guilt, shame, doubt, and self-effort. As these are peeled off by the grace of God made real by the Spirit of God and activated by the people of God, those who have come out can really begin to live! That's what happened to me, and I hope that's what's happening to you . . . even at this moment.

In religion, we try harder to live up to God's standards so we get to live longer in eternity. How dry and empty is that? The Christian life isn't just an extension of our old life with a few fringe benefits and a lot of hard work. Our old life has died with Christ, and we have a new life in Him!

The Christian life isn't just an extension of our old life with a few fringe benefits and a lot of hard work.

Jesus wanted to make sure the people listening to Him understood that He wasn't just offering a slightly better system of religious activity. The Pharisees were upset because He didn't fit in their boxes. In response, Jesus exploded the boxes! He used an illustration they could easily understand. In those days, wine wasn't kept in bottles; it was aged in skins. But the skins shrank as the wine aged, so it they weren't usable for new wine. He explained:

> "No one sews a patch of unshrunk cloth on an old garment, for the patch will pull away from the garment, making the tear worse. Neither do people pour new wine into old wineskins. If they do, the skins will burst; the wine will run out and the wineskins will be ruined. No, they pour new wine into new wineskins, and both are preserved." (Matthew 9:16-17)

For much of my life, I tried to put the new wine of God's love into the old wineskin of performance, comparison, and shame. It burst and made a mess over and over again! The new wine of God's amazing grace needs to be put in the new wineskin of the truth that we're dead, raised, and ascended in Christ. "The old has passed away. Behold, the new has come!"

Some will ask, "But Ben, what happens when I don't feel this union with Jesus?"

Great question. We're humans, not robots. Our emotions are fickle and often bewildering. We need to unhitch our confidence from our feelings and connect it to the truths we're studying in this book. The gospel of grace doesn't ebb and flow with our feelings. It's the rock that never changes because Jesus is the rock who always loves, always cares, and always delights in us. Believe it, whether you feel it or not, and you'll feel it more than you used to. I guarantee it.

Come out of the jungle. Use the new wineskins filled with the new wine of grace as treatment for PTRSD.

DECLARATION:

Jesus, You've done everything to bring me into
perfect union with You.

CONSIDER THIS:

1.   Do you know anyone who relates to God like the people at the foot at Mt. Sinai? Have you ever related to God that way? Explain your answer.

2.   What are some ways Jesus' connections with people were different from the Israelites' experience at Mt. Sinai?

3. How would you explain Paul's point about the difference between "the works of the flesh" and "the fruit of the Spirit"?

4. Does it offend you or encourage you that Paul said we use a primal cry for God: "Abba"? Explain your answer.

5. Why are old wineskins of performance more attractive to some people than the new wineskins of grace?

CHAPTER 6

ENDLESS PENANCE

DIRTY VS. RIGHTEOUS

WE'VE SEEN HOW THE SACRIFICE OF CHRIST HAS GIVEN US complete forgiveness. That's an incredible and wonderful gift! But justification, "to be made right with God," actually has two components: the *death of Christ* imputed to us has, indeed, paid for all of our sins: past, present, and future, and *the life of Christ* imparted to us gives us His own righteousness. This is the gospel swap: Jesus takes our sins and we get His righteousness! Paul explains this clearly in two passages. To the Corinthians, he wrote, "God made [Jesus] who had no sin to be sin for us, so that in him we might become the righteousness of God" (2 Corinthians 5:21). And to the believers in the Greek city of Philippi, he explained that the things other people pursue are meaningless to him because the death of Jesus has freed him from comparison, competition, and jealousy, but he's not empty; he's full!

But whatever were gains to me I now consider loss for the sake
of Christ. What is more, I consider everything a loss because
of the surpassing worth of knowing Christ Jesus my Lord, for
whose sake I have lost all things. I consider them garbage, that
I may gain Christ and be found in him, not having a righteousness of my own that comes from the law, but that which is
through faith in Christ—the righteousness that comes from
God on the basis of faith. (Philippians 3:7-9)

Could the law make someone righteous? My goodness, if anyone
could become righteous by being obedient to the law, the Jewish leaders in the days of Jesus and Paul certainly would have been, but their
rigidity only made them like the grouchy elder brother in Jesus' story
of the prodigal. They were self-righteous (which is the exact opposite
of Christ's righteousness), angry, defiant, and bitter. That's not the
grace-filled life Jesus offers us! No, the law is powerless to make anyone
righteous, but the gospel can and does. At the beginning of Paul's mon-
umental letter to the Christians in Rome, he lays out his central point:

For I am not ashamed of the gospel, because it is the power of
God that brings salvation to everyone who believes: first to the
Jew, then to the Gentile. For in the gospel the righteousness
of God is revealed—a righteousness that is by faith from first
to last, just as it is written: "The righteous will live by faith."
(Romans 1:16-17)

Justification—forgiveness and righteousness—is received, not
earned. Both aspects are ours when we trust in Jesus.

MORE THAN WE CAN IMAGINE

When I ask people in church if they're righteous, a few try to ac-
knowledge the fact that Jesus has made them righteous, but most
instantly insist, "No way, Pastor!" They're looking at their experience,
their lifestyle, their behavior, and they conclude they're too dirty to be
considered clean and righteous. But they're looking at themselves in
the mirror "in their sight." We need to see ourselves "in God's sight,"
and He has declared us righteous. How righteous? He has imparted to
us the very righteousness of Christ . . . perfect righteousness. You don't
believe me?

Two chapters later in Paul's letter, he pulls out the big guns and
contrasts the effects of the law and the effects of grace:

> Now we know that whatever the law says, it says to those who
> are under the law, so that every mouth may be silenced and the
> whole world held accountable to God. Therefore no one will
> be declared righteous in God's sight by the works of the law;
> rather, through the law we become conscious of our sin.
>
> But now apart from the law the righteousness of God has
> been made known, to which the Law and the Prophets testify.
> This righteousness is given through faith in Jesus Christ to all
> who believe. There is no difference between Jew and Gentile,
> for all have sinned and fall short of the glory of God, and all are
> justified freely by his grace through the redemption that came
> by Christ Jesus. (Romans 3:19-24)

This, my friend, is the good news! We can stop trying to earn God's
love and acceptance, and feeling so dirty because we fail so miserably,
and we can hold out our hands and receive the free gift of grace, a grace
that takes away our sin and replaces it with the status of Christ's perfect

life. When God sees you, this is what He sees: a pure, spotless son or daughter who has the same standing before Him as Jesus—not that we're the unique, uncreated Son of God, but all of His compassion, obedience, love, and purity is credited to our account.

When God sees you, this is what He sees: a pure, spotless son or daughter who has the same standing before Him as Jesus— all of His compassion, obedience, love, and purity is credited to our account.

To be sure, our behavior and attitudes don't measure up to the perfection of Jesus. We fall way, way short. That's how most of us look at ourselves, but it's not how God looks at us. This is the wonder of the gospel. This is why those who get it are overwhelmed with the extravagant grace of God. We who are undeserving are recipients of His magnificent love, and He has given us something we could never earn: we're justified, made right with God.

In another of Paul's letters, this one to the Colossians, he includes a prayer for them in the opening. Half of the prayer is gratitude for God's grace. That seems about right to me. If we have any grasp of the gospel, that's how much time we'll want to praise and thank Him. If they experience grace, Paul writes, they will give "joyful thanks to the Father, who has qualified you to share in the inheritance of his holy people in the kingdom of light. For he has rescued us from the dominion of darkness and brought us into the kingdom of the Son he loves, in whom we have redemption, the forgiveness of sins" (Colossians 1:12-14). Notice that the Father has *qualified* us to share in all the benefits of redemption.

That must mean that we were *disqualified* before the gospel changed everything in us and for us. Joyful thanks is the only appropriate response for those who were outside being brought inside, for those who had no hope now having a living hope, and for those who were dirty but are now cleansed.

SHAME AND MISPLACED ZEAL

As I've pastored thousands of people over the years, I've noticed two unhealthy responses to the twin truths found in justification. Some can't believe it and continue to live in shame, and others really don't think they need it because they're doing so many things for God.

Sensitive, reflective people and those who have been deeply hurt are vulnerable to the conclusion that they're still helpless, hopeless, and worthless even after they've trusted in Christ. They've tried so hard, but they've hurt so bad. These are the friends who can't accept a compliment, those who are afraid to express an opinion because others might disagree, and those who retreat into a private world where no one can hurt them again. They read and hear about the magnificent love of God, but they assume it's for other people, not them. They live with an undercurrent of self-pity, with occasional spikes of anger. But the anger makes them feel out of control, so they put the clamps on their emotions more tightly than ever. It's not that they don't believe God is loving, strong, and wise, but they think they're too far gone to experience His grace.

But there are plenty of Pharisees in our churches today. No, they don't wear long robes and sandals, but they act much like the religious leaders of the first century. The Pharisees were very devout, they never missed a Sabbath, and they made up extra laws to prove they were completely dedicated to God. They looked down at "those people" who weren't as obedient and felt completely superior. Instead of self-pity, they felt self-righteous. Today, when modern Pharisees hear the gospel message of unmerited grace, they claim God's love as their right because they secretly are sure they deserve it. "After all," they conclude as they look at people who aren't as dedicated and devout, "I'm not like them!"

Later in Paul's letter to the Romans, he addresses those whose strict obedience actually keeps them from experiencing the love of God:

> Brothers and sisters, my heart's desire and prayer to God for the Israelites is that they may be saved. For I can testify about them that they are zealous for God, but their zeal is not based on knowledge. Since they did not know the righteousness of God and sought to establish their own, they did not submit to God's righteousness. Christ is the culmination of the law so that there may be righteousness for everyone who believes. (Romans 10:1-4)

Plenty of people try to prove their value to God by their zeal—their passion and activism—but with it comes an implicit condemnation of those who aren't as zealous. Do you doubt there are people like that in the church today? If you do, you need to open your eyes and look around. Jesus spoke harsh correction to the religious leaders of His day, but it was always because He loved them and wanted them to experience grace. If you recall the end of Jesus' story of the father and the two sons, the story ends with the father going out to the older son (who represents the religious elite who were standing around Him as He talked to the "tax collectors and sinners"), and the father pleads with him to come to the celebration of salvation. He doesn't say, "You ingrate!" or "You fool!" He tenderly says, "My son," which in the original language is actually, "My child." Through the father in the story, Jesus was gently, lovingly inviting the Pharisees to "come to their senses," give up their pride, and humble themselves to accept God's grace. How did they respond? Only weeks later, they launched their plot to kill Him.

I'm not saying that some people in the church want to kill Jesus, but it's indisputable that some are like the religious elite who refused to humble themselves to gratefully receive grace because they believed they could earn God's favor. They had zeal but no knowledge of the beauty and the power of the gospel.

Some of these people work so hard for so long that they become utterly exhausted. They wonder, *Was all this worth it? I've obeyed. Why don't I experience more love from God?* At that moment, they have some choices: to double down and work even harder, give up and drift to the edges of the church community, or realize they've missed God's heart all those years. These are the three options I faced for many years. As a pastor, I couldn't drift away. I believed that my emptiness and feeling dirty could be fixed by being more zealous, but it was a disaster! For those years, I preached as hard as I could, but the love of God felt far away. Finally—thank God!—He opened my eyes to the wonder of grace, and my life hasn't been the same.

At that moment, they have some choices: to double down and work even harder, give up and drift to the edges of the church community, or realize they've missed God's heart all those years.

God gives grace to the humble, but only the humble want it. Those who continue in shame are sure they know more than God about how life works, and they believe feeling terrible about themselves somehow earns points with God. And those who depend on their zeal don't believe they need grace. Oh, they're glad Jesus died for them so they have a ticket to heaven, but the love of God hasn't penetrated their hard hearts. The first group feels perpetually inferior; the other perpetually superior . . . and neither one has experiential knowledge of God's grace, love, and kindness. Humble people see their crying need for grace, and they know they can't earn it. Over and over again, the Scriptures shout that justification—complete forgiveness and Christ's righteousness—is a gift. Sooner or later, at least some people believe it!

CONVICTION

I've often heard (and I've often said), "Man, I'm under such conviction. I need to repent and get right with God." It sounds very spiritual and humble, doesn't it? To be honest, that's been the teaching of the church for generations. Let me pose a different way to think.

On the night Jesus was betrayed, He spent time with His disciples between their meal together and the arrest. He had a lot to tell them! One of the most important was that another Advocate was coming. (I'm sure it had already blown their minds that Jesus claimed to be equal to the Father, and now He was introducing another person who was God!) To explain the role of the Holy Spirit, Jesus explained, "When he comes, he will prove the world to be in the wrong about sin and righteousness and judgment: about sin, because people do not believe in me; about righteousness, because I am going to the Father, where you can see me no longer; and about judgment, because the prince of this world now stands condemned" (John 16:8-11). The Spirit convicts the world of sin, not sins. What is that sin? It's unbelief, the sin under all other sins. And who does He convict of sin? The world. And who does He convict of righteousness? Believers! This is similar to Paul's assertion that the Holy Spirit testifies with our spirits that we're children of

God. The Spirit convicts, or assures, us that at Pentecost and beyond, His coming changed people from the inside out. And now, we can all have the certainty of God's forgiveness, the certainty that Christ's righteousness has been credited to us, and the certainty that the love and power of Jesus has been unleashed in us. The Holy Spirit isn't a mean third-grade teacher who points out every flaw every minute of every day. He shares the heart of the Father and the Son, full of compassion and kindness, reminding us again and again that we belong, we're safe, and we're cleansed. He sees Jesus in us.

But there's a third conviction: judgment against "the prince of this world." Our enemy is called "the accuser" because he stands in the courtroom blasting us with accusations about our sins. The sensitive among us are crushed, the insensitive among us blame somebody else, and some of us are so gifted that we find a way to do both! We need to pay attention to the text. Jesus is saying that the Holy Spirit's role isn't to judge us, but to judge Satan. We're not the object of God's condemnation; the enemy is. We're not the ones who need to live in fear of punishment; Satan is.

Does this view of the Holy Spirit's role matter? Yes, in a huge way! His conviction of unbelief reminds us of the chief sin that Jesus has forgiven by His blood, His conviction of the righteousness granted to each believer gives us stability and confidence, and His conviction that Satan is judged, not us, assures us that the only way God treats us is with immeasurable affection.

Far too many of us live under the specter of God's condemnation. We assume He's watching and waiting for us to say or do something that's displeasing so He can lower the boom. Our relationship with Him is based on fear, not love. Our greatest hope is to avoid getting clobbered with guilt and shame, and someday, escape all this by going to heaven . . . where we hope God doesn't remember how mad at us He was!

In John's first letter and in Paul's letter to Titus, we read that the experience of forgiveness and the gift of righteousness melt our hearts so we delight in God and obey Him from the motive of gratitude. We're not always looking over our shoulder to see if God is going to get us for doing something wrong, but rather looking into the eyes of the One who loves us so much that He gave everything to bring us close.

Some of us are too timid, and we need the security of the truth that God has granted us Christ's righteousness. And some of us are too brash, and we need the humility of knowing it's a gift, not something we earned.

Some of us are too timid, and we need the security of the truth that God has granted us Christ's righteousness. And some of us are too brash, and we need the humility of knowing it's a gift, not something we earned. When we dive deeper into the gospel, we see things that have been there all along but we haven't noticed. For instance, in Romans 5, Paul contrasts Adam and Jesus: one brought sin, the other brought salvation; one started with a single sin, the other paid the price for all sins. But righteousness is also part of the picture. Paul almost shouted, "For if, by the trespass of the one man, death reigned through that one man, how much more will those who receive God's abundant provision of grace and of the gift of righteousness reign in life through the one man, Jesus Christ!" (Romans 5:17) Did you get it? We who have received the abundant provision of grace and righteousness "reign in life" through Jesus. Reigning in life is much more than barely getting by. It's far better than thinking God tolerates us. It's much more powerful than meager self-dependence. It has a far higher purpose than barely making it to tomorrow. We reign with Jesus. He is on the throne next to the Father, and we're in Him on the same throne.

When we see ourselves the way God sees us, we expect good things from our Father, we trust that He'll use hard times for good purposes, and we'll rest in the security of His love. That's what it means to be an "overcomer." We overcome through the gospel, not by gritting our teeth and trying our best to hang in there. We overcome because Christ's death and life have been credited to our accounts. We stand on the Rock, and we're filled with all the fullness of God.

For many of us, righteousness seems like a stiff word, lacking in warmth. In fact, for many, the mention of the word reminds us that we were terribly unrighteous, leading to guilt, fear, shame, and denial. But when we see it as one of the supreme gifts from God, that it's a measure of His immense love, it's no longer cold and demanding. We get a glimpse of how it changes us in Paul's letter to the Colossians. Holiness and righteousness are closely connected. Paul encourages believers to see themselves the way God sees them, and if they do, they'll act the way God acts toward us:

> Therefore, as God's chosen people, holy and dearly loved, clothe yourselves with compassion, kindness, humility, gentleness and patience. Bear with each other and forgive one another if any of you has a grievance against someone. Forgive as the Lord forgave you. And over all these virtues put on love, which binds them all together in perfect unity.

Let the peace of Christ rule in your hearts, since as members of one body you were called to peace. And be thankful. Let the message of Christ dwell among you richly as you teach and admonish one another with all wisdom through psalms, hymns, and songs from the Spirit, singing to God with gratitude in your hearts. And whatever you do, whether in word or deed, do it all in the name of the Lord Jesus, giving thanks to God the Father through him. (Colossians 3:12-17)

Isn't that the life you want? Sure it is, or you wouldn't have read this far in the book. Isn't this the kind of impact you want the gospel to have on you? Of course. Isn't this how you want to relate to the people around you? Indeed. This is a picture of what it looks like to reign in life. This is the result of being convinced that we're in Christ in His death and in Him in His perfect, righteous life. That's the gift of God. Embrace it. Believe it. Live it.

DECLARATION:

By sheer grace, Christ's righteousness,
His perfect life, has been credited to me.

CONSIDER THIS:

1. How would you describe "the gospel swap"?

2. Before you read this chapter, how would you have responded if someone asked, "Are you righteous?" How would you respond now?

3. In what way is shame an attempt to compensate for feeling dirty? What does it promise? Why doesn't it work to control people?

4. Why do you think "misplaced zeal" is so attractive and powerful? How is it deadly?

5. Describe the Holy Spirit's role in convicting people.

6. What does it (or will it) mean for you to "reign in life"?

CHAPTER 7

AN ORPHAN MENTALITY

VICTIM VS. VICTOR

THE TITLE OF THIS CHAPTER ISN'T MEANT TO DISPARAGE ANYONE. I'm not saying that orphans are less valuable or somehow defective. I only want to use some characteristics that are common to those whose parents have died or abandoned them. Actually, some of the most successful people of all time were orphans whose grit and determination drove them to excel, including First Lady Eleanor Roosevelt, Apple's Steve Jobs, and Olympic gymnast Simone Biles.[16] Still, psychologists have noted some common, detremental traits among those who have lost both parents.[17] We begin, however, with Jesus assuring His closest followers that He wouldn't abandon them.

On the night He was betrayed, Jesus spoke a couple of times about the promise of the Holy Spirit. I'm sure the disciples were perplexed with all they were hearing. Jesus told them He was going away. They had been with Him day and night for over three years, and now He was announcing He was leaving them! (In fact, He had told them many times before, but they didn't get it.) Jesus assured them the "Spirit of truth" would come, and He promised them: " I will not leave you as orphans; I will come to you. Before long, the world will not see me anymore, but you will see me. Because I live, you also will live" (John 14:18-19). He packed a lot into those sentences, and they wouldn't understand until a few days later on Easter morning. Jesus' arrest, trial, and execution would shatter their confidence, but they wouldn't be left high and dry. He promised to appear again after the resurrection, and then, He would impart to them His resurrection life. But there was more to His new teaching about the presence of God: Jesus had walked *beside* them; the Holy Spirit would live *inside* them!

As they listened, the disciples feared abandonment, but Jesus assured them they were sons of the Father. They were going to be frightened during the events of the next few hours and days, but He promised the presence of the Spirit of God.

I understand their fear. I grew up with wonderful parents, but somewhere along the way, I developed an orphan mindset. As I've gone deeper into the gospel of grace over the past eight years, God has progressively shown me areas of my life that hadn't yet been touched by His truth and power. One of those is what this chapter is about. I have so much to be thankful for: a beautiful and loving wife, terrific kids, great friends, good health, a defining purpose, and the best people in the world who serve at our church . . . but I had seen myself as a victim. I saw every good thing as arbitrary and temporary: "Well, this isn't going to last." And I saw every difficulty through the lens of grievance: "This isn't fair! Doesn't anybody care? Doesn't anybody understand?"

The Spirit showed me that I had lived that way most of my life. (I'm sure Kim tried to tell me a thousand times, but I wouldn't listen. Go figure.) I realized I'd been blaming people for every problem, and I saw problems where none existed. I assumed that everyone was against me and out to get me, so I had to be on guard all the time. (Psychologists call this "hyper-vigilance.") I questioned others' motives because I was cynical about anyone having good intentions. I was constantly self-focused, like a schizophrenic, sometimes bludgeoning myself with harsh condemnation and other times trying to look good so people would think well of me—either way, it was all about me. Comparison was my constant companion. I compared myself to pastors, CEOs, and those in other leadership positions, always checking out where I stood in light of their success and mine. I felt driven to climb the ladder of success, and too often I used people as steppingstones instead of loving them as the sheep God had entrusted to my care.

I realized I'd been blaming people for every problem, and I saw problems where none existed. I assumed that everyone was against me and out to get me, so I had to be on guard all the time.

One morning God woke me up at about 3 o'clock and revealed this pattern of thinking, living, and relating, and He assured me that I didn't have to live that way any longer. I could walk in the victory of being His beloved, royal son. I already knew the truth of my identity, but I needed to apply it more deeply and specifically. He convinced me that my misunderstanding and unbelief hadn't changed His view of me. He wasn't casting me out. Instead, He was revealing more of His grace to me. His kindness, not His wrath, was calling me to repentance.

Here's my point: this chapter is, to a large extent, a big part of my testimony of God infusing His grace more deeply into my life. I've been learning, more than ever, to walk in the grace God has showered on me, and I want to share what I've learned.

THE CONTRAST

Many Christians live like orphans instead of children of the King. Unloved orphans sense a deep emptiness. They may be afraid they won't get the next meal or have a place to sleep that night. They grasp at whatever they can reach, and when they get it, they won't let go. They feel isolated because they either have been or are alone—physically, emotionally, and psychologically. When they look around, they see everyone else as competition for meager resources, and they've concluded that authority figures are disinterested. They often believe there's something very wrong with them—and that's the reason no one wants them. Even after they're adopted into loving homes, the mindset of deficit continues for months and even years . . . and some never get over the deeply ingrained sense of desperation and loneliness. Shame, self-pity, and resentment often cloud their minds, turn their hearts into deserts, and ruin their relationships.

But those who realize they are royal children sense their Father's love. They feel secure, confident, and boldly creative. They're willing to take risks because they know failure can't harm their Father's view of them, and they're vulnerable because they're sure the Father knows everything about them and loves them dearly. They realize their Father has limitless resources which He's happy to share. If they experience any lack, they don't wonder if the Father still loves them; they're convinced He has a good reason for any deficit or delay. They trust His heart even when they don't see the work of His hands.

When the five thousand men and their families were hungry after listening to Jesus preach, the disciples panicked because they couldn't figure out how to feed the crowd. They were acting like orphans. For the Son, though, it was no problem. A couple of fish and some little loaves of bread? That's plenty to produce a feast by the power of God.

Orphans manipulate people to get what they want. They shade the truth (that's called lying) and twist people into knots to put pressure on them. But children of God "love without hypocrisy" (Romans 12:9 NASB). They speak the truth and let people make up their own minds . . . and live with the consequences.

Orphans are weak, but they often cover it by appearing tough and strong. In contrast, the King's kids are genuinely strong and secure, so they can serve with gentleness and humility. Orphans are always grasping for more, but God's beloved children have full hearts and open hands in generosity. Orphans are either demanding, defiant, or depressed; the King's children are joyful and grateful.

Author and cultural analyst Joseph Mattera has written about the stark contrasts between believers who have an orphan mentality, which he calls an "orphan spirit," and those who are convinced they are the King's beloved children. I want to highlight just two of them:

- *The orphan spirit operates out of insecurity and jealousy. The spirit of sonship functions out of love and acceptance.*

Those with an orphan spirit are constantly battling jealousy and insecurity since security originates in a secure relationship with our parents. Those with an orphan spirit are so insecure they even have a hard time hearing a biological or spiritual father praise their siblings or co-laborers. Those with the spirit of sonship are so secure in the Father's love and favor that they are content to serve in any capacity needed, whether or not they are in charge or are celebrated in the process.

• *The orphan spirit receives their primary identity through material possessions, their physical appearance, and activities. The spirit of sonship has their identity grounded in their sonship and their Father's affirmation.*

Those with an orphan spirit can never have enough career success, material possessions, pleasure, or illicit relationships to satisfy the hole in their heart related to their identity. Consequently, they are constantly striving to gain satisfaction through the use of various things or people in their lives. In many cases even their [appearance] can be their way of trying to stand out as unique and a cry for attention due to a lack of self-esteem and fatherly affirmation.

Those who walk in sonship are so grounded in their divine Father's affirmation they can be satisfied serving in the background and celebrate the success and attention that others receive because the void in their soul has already been filled with the unconditional love of the Father.[18]

REVELATION

I find great comfort in the psalmist's story in Psalm 73. Asaph was furious. He was angry with God because life wasn't fair. He had obeyed God, trusted God, and been faithful to God, but "the arrogant" and "the wicked" were getting ahead of him in the game of life. He went to great lengths to describe what he was upset about: they didn't struggle, they were rich, and they didn't have to wrestle with sickness. They were peacocks of pride, showing off all their wealth, and worse, "they clothe themselves with violence" without any consequences. They were getting off scot-free! They scoffed at people who were trying to live a God-honoring life (like Asaph!), and they claimed to be outside any judgment of God. They wondered out loud, "How would God know? Does the Most High know anything?" (Psalm 73:11)

This wasn't a momentary mood for Asaph. He resented the lavish, easy life of the wicked rich people, and he resented God's apparent abandonment. He concluded:

Surely in vain I have kept my heart pure
    and have washed my hands in innocence.
All day long I have been afflicted,
    and every morning brings new punishments. (vv. 13-14)

In other words, "God, it's not worth it to follow You! It doesn't pay off like I thought it would." But God showed up with a revelation about the destiny of the ungodly and His ultimate aim for His children. I appreciate Asaph's brutal honesty as he describes the turning point:

When my heart was grieved
    and my spirit embittered,
I was senseless and ignorant;
    I was a brute beast before you.
Yet I am always with you;
    you hold me by my right hand.
You guide me with your counsel,
    and afterward you will take me into glory.
Whom have I in heaven but you?
    And earth has nothing I desire besides you.

My flesh and my heart may fail,
>> but God is the strength of my heart
>> and my portion forever. (vv. 21-26)

When Asaph was at his worst, like "a brute beast," God didn't pull away, and He didn't slap His doubting child. Oh no. In exquisite tenderness, He took Asaph's hand. At that moment, everything changed for him. Instead of seeing himself as an orphan, he saw himself as a beloved son of God. And he responded to God's love with trust, wonder, and confidence in the future. It's one of the most radical transformations in the Scriptures. How did it happen? Asaph poured his heart out to God, and God poured His heart into Asaph.

How did it happen? Asaph poured his heart out to God, and God poured His heart into Asaph.

GOD'S KINGDOM, NOT OURS

Peter wrote to believers who had experienced severe persecution in Palestine and had fled to safer parts of the Roman Empire. They *felt* like exiles because they *were* exiles, but Peter had a galvanizing message for them. He reminded them of their new identity in Christ: "But you are a chosen people, a royal priesthood, a holy nation, God's special possession, that you may declare the praises of him who called you out of darkness into his wonderful light. Once you were not a people, but now you are the people of God; once you had not received mercy, but now you have received mercy" (1 Peter 2:9-10).

What did it mean for them to walk in this identity in a multicultural country where the forces of authority weren't very sympathetic to their faith? Does this question sound vaguely familiar? I believe God wants us to ask the same question today: How can we be "a royal priesthood, a holy nation, God's special possession" and "declare the praises of him who has called us out of darkness" to the people around us? Jesus came "full of grace and truth," not one or the other, and He calls His people to walk in the same tension. In our bitterly polarized society, I'm afraid I see far more Christians despising those who disagree with them (even other brothers and sisters in Christ) than loving them in spite of their differences. We don't have to agree with people to love them. Jesus certainly didn't agree with the sinners, tax collectors, and Pharisees, but He loved them to death.

I'm afraid we're losing the younger generation in this country who see us living with an orphan mentality instead of boldly living and loving like Jesus. Don't get me wrong: I'm not saying we need to lower our standards or change our policy positions just so we can get along—that's not genuine love; it's only compliance. Jesus held to the truth and loved to the uttermost. Can we follow His example? Or maybe a better question is: What does it say about our grasp of grace if we can't have calm, respectful conversations with people on the other side? Do we love Democrats? Do we love Republicans? Do we love people who are more moderate than we are? Do we love the people who march for Black Lives Matter? Do we love the police? Do we reach out to heal hurts, or do we stand back and watch people suffer? Do we step in to call for justice, or do we delight in condemning people because they don't believe exactly like us or look exactly like us?

As the 2016 election neared, sociologist Arlie Russell Hochschild was finishing her study of blue collar families in Louisiana. She observed that a seismic shift had been taking place in our country. For years, hardworking people had been trying to get ahead, to get their slice of the American dream, but they felt others who were less deserving had been "cutting in line" ahead of them. The men and women in her study felt like victims—unwanted and left behind, like they didn't belong. She titled her book *Strangers in Their Own Land.* She notes:

> Not only have the country's two main political parties split further apart on such issues, but political feeling also runs deeper than it did in the past. In 1960, when a survey asked American adults whether it would "disturb" them if their child married a member of the other political party, no more than 5 percent of either party answered "yes." But in 2010, 33 percent of Democrats and 40 percent of Republicans answered "yes." In fact, *partyism*, as some call it, now beats race as the source of divisive prejudice.
>
> Our polarization, and the increasing reality that we simply don't know each other, makes it too easy to settle for dislike and contempt.[19]

A few years ago, author Charles Sykes wrote a book called *A Nation of Victims.* He was referring to the way people are quick to sue each other instead of resolving disputes outside the courtroom. The title of his book would be perfect to describe the heart, agendas, and behavior of most people in our country today, but the problem is much bigger now. People are acting like helpless, furious victims about virtually every issue. Is that a fair analysis? Let me ask a few questions: Do people fear that our country is changing? Sure. Are there inequalities? Obviously. Are some people taking advantage of the system while others are being left behind? That's the conclusion of many, and they're right at least to some degree and in some cases. These issues (and many others) need to be addressed, but not with whining and venom . . . at least for Christians. We have an incredible opportunity to step into the fray with love and patience, seeking to understand before we're understood, listening before speaking, and providing comfort for those who are on the other side of the cultural divide. That's what Jesus did for you and me, and that's what He's calling us to do in our world today.

Where do you get your news? How do you use social media? How many very good conversations have you had in the past week with people who disagree with you? (And a "very good conversation" doesn't mean they caved in and now agree with you!) Take an inventory of your speech, your posts, your input of news, and your heart. Are you any different in your language from those who don't know God?

A friend of mine leads a group with a number of couples who are quite politically partisan. They have had very, very strong opinions about our last few presidents, and they feel completely confident everyone should agree with them. My friend has tried to steer the conversation to valuing the principles of God's kingdom over either political party, and recently, he asked simply, "Jesus told us to love our enemies. What does it mean to love people on the other side . . . or people on your side who aren't as committed as you are?" A few of the couples looked at each other like they'd had similar conversations between them, but no one said a word. No one admitted that genuine, robust love is more important than political ideology.

We'll be incredibly patient with those who disagree with us, which is at least half of the people in the country. And we'll communicate God's truth, the gospel, more passionately than any political position.

Surely we can do better than that. If the grace of Jesus has changed our hearts, we'll be more like Him. We'll love the people He loves, which is everybody. We'll be incredibly patient with those who disagree with us, which is at least half of the people in the country. And we'll communicate God's truth, the gospel, more passionately than any political position.

How are you doing with that?

Are we any different from unbelievers? Are our marriages stronger, our children happier, our finances more solid, and our relationships more loving? In too many cases, the answer is "no." It's no wonder people look at us and ask, "What gives you the right to tell me how to live?" We don't have the right; we earn the right to be heard. Here's how . . .

Paul gave a series of instructions to the Romans:

- "Accept the one whose faith is weak, without quarreling over disputable matters" (Romans 14:1). The "weak" aren't the people most of us expect. A weak person in Paul's mind isn't someone who is indecisive; it's someone who is rigidly dogmatic. We're to accept this defiant, demanding person with kindness and avoid the usual quarrels.

- "If we live, we live for the Lord; and if we die, we die for the Lord. So, whether we live or die, we belong to the Lord. For this very reason, Christ died and returned to life so that he might be the Lord of both the dead and the living. You, then, why do you judge your brother or sister? Or why do you treat them with contempt? For we will all stand before God's judgment seat" (vv. 8-10). Some things are more important than being right in an argument! Treating people with contempt is to despise them for what they believe.

- "For the kingdom of God is not a matter of eating and drinking, but of righteousness, peace and joy in the Holy Spirit" (v. 17). When we value God's kingdom over our preferences, we join Jesus in praying, "Your kingdom come, your will be done on earth as it is in heaven." His kingdom is built on the foundation of kindness, righteousness, and justice. (See Jeremiah 9:23-24.)

- "Let us therefore make every effort to do what leads to peace and to mutual edification" (v. 19). It takes work to be a peacemaker and build people up instead of tearing them down.

Our public witness is at stake. Actually, it's always at stake, but it seems that this season in our nation's history is especially tense. Jesus called us to be light and salt—light to bring the truth of the gospel and the kindness of God to a dark, angry, polarized world, and salt as a flavoring and a preservative. I'm worried that the flavor people taste when they're near us isn't the sweetness of grace, peace, and joy.

Let's be honest. Some of you have just concluded that I've lost my mind and no one should pay attention to me any longer. Here's what I'm trying to say: I'm not advocating that we be Republican Christians or Democrat Christians; I'm pleading that we become Kingdom Christians—first, foremost, deeply, and always. When we see ourselves as victims (of the right or the left), we live with an orphan mentality. We complain, we blame, and we vent our anger at those who are "out to get us." That's not how Jesus responded to people who disagreed with Him. He moved toward them, invited them to spend time with Him, and shared His heart with them. And if they still didn't agree, He didn't stop loving them. My hope is that believers will become so enraptured with the deep, transforming truths of God's grace that we're known for our love, not our political stances; for our compassion, not our resentment; and for our patience, not for blaming others for every problem. While the kingdom of God isn't *of* this world, it's certainly *for* this world. It must affect us personally and flow through us to have positive impact on everyone everywhere we go. I'm afraid we have become part of the problem, but we can do something about it. We can repent of our orphan mentality and let the love of Jesus give us the security and compassion we need to relate to all kinds of people in this troubled world.

If you want to bark back at me, go to #PastorBenWhatInThe-WorldAreYouThinking? (Just kidding, but I welcome your feedback and insights.)

Like Asaph . . . and like me . . . all of us need to recognize our orphan mentality in order to do anything about it. And like the psalmist, we can pour out our frustrations, our bitterness, and our self-pity to God. He can handle it. And we can be sure He'll take our hand, remind us of His love and our new identity, and guide us in a much better path.

DECLARATION:

I'm a victor in Christ, not a victim.

CONSIDER THIS:

1. What are characteristics of an orphan mentality?

2. What are characteristics of a son or daughter of the King?

3. Has there been a time when you would have identified with Asaph in his self-pity and resentment? If so, what was happening? How did you resolve your heart problem (if, in fact, it has been resolved)?

4. Were you offended or encouraged to read the part of the chapter about living for God's kingdom in a polarized society? Explain your answer.

5. Do you need to make any changes to follow Paul's instructions to the Romans? If so, what are they? When and how will you do them? What difference will it make?

CHAPTER 8

RIGHTLY DIVIDING

BEFORE VS. AFTER

I'M CONVINCED THAT THE BIGGEST REASON I STAYED STUCK IN the jungle so long was that I failed to understand one of the principal themes in the Bible. Throughout the Scriptures, we find God making covenants with His people. We usually think of Moses coming down from Mt. Sinai with the Ten Commandments, but there are many others. God made a covenant with Adam, Noah, Abraham, Moses, and David. All of those looked forward to the greatest covenant, the New Covenant inaugurated in Jesus. In Paul's second letter to Timothy, he wrote, "Be diligent to present yourself approved to God, a worker who does not need to be ashamed, rightly dividing the word of truth" (2 Timothy 2:15 NKJV). That's exactly the point: we need to rightly divide the old covenants from the new covenant, what happened *before* the cross from what happened *after* it.

The promise of the Old Testament covenants was that a new day was coming. Everything God was doing for, in, and through the nation of Israel was preparing them for the Messiah who would fulfill all the promises ... and more! We certainly have glimpses of God's grace in the Old Testament, but they are often partial and conditional. Something far better was coming. God spoke through Ezekiel:

> "I will sprinkle clean water on you, and you will be clean; I will cleanse you from all your impurities and from all your idols. I will give you a new heart and put a new spirit in you; I will remove from you your heart of stone and give you a heart of flesh. And I will put my Spirit in you and move you to follow my decrees and be careful to keep my laws." (Ezekiel 36:25-27)

Our connection with God would no longer be external and dependent on our obedience; it would become internal and based on Jesus' obedience. How obedient? Paul probably quotes a first-century hymn in his letter to the Philippians. It describes the deity and humility of Jesus the Christ:

> Who, being in very nature God,
> > did not consider equality with God something to be used
> > to his own advantage;
> rather, he made himself nothing
> > by taking the very nature of a servant,
> > being made in human likeness.
> And being found in appearance as a man,
> > he humbled himself
> > by becoming obedient to death—
> > even death on a cross! (Philippians 2:6-8)

The cross changes everything! That's the moment the veil was ripped in two, an earthquake opened tombs and the dead came back to life, and death was defeated. Those who believe in Jesus have a heart transplant: their heart of stone is replaced with a tender heart for God.

For too long, I had straddled the fence with one foot in the Old Covenant and the other in the New. No longer. I jumped into the new!

For too long, I had straddled the fence with one foot in the Old Covenant and the other in the New. No longer. I jumped into the new!

(Note: In the last three chapters, we'll review the truths we've already examined and see how we can apply them more specifically each day.)

WHAT DOES THE BIBLE SAY?

When I read the Bible and preached from it, I noted plenty of commands and warnings, but I also saw evidence of God's grace. I whipsawed from one to the other, feeling compelled to live up to God's standards to prove myself, but wondering how that fit with the passages that describe God's limitless love. I was confused, and I'm quite sure I confused plenty of people listening to me.

At one point I read *Knowing and Experiencing God* by Arthur Meintjes. When I read his story, I instantly identified. He points to the verse in 2 Timothy and writes:

For most of my Christian life, I believed this verse to mean, "Study the scriptures to prove to God that you are a workman that needs not to be ashamed." To me it meant that I must study the Word faithfully and diligently. This work of regularly studying the Bible would prove to God that I am a good student of His Word, someone who is really seeking Him. By doing this, I could demonstrate to God that I really am willing and obedient to Him. Then I would be able to rightly divide the Word of Truth. This is how many others interpret and understand this passage of Scripture.

As Meintjes studied this verse, however, God led him to a very different conclusion: We don't study to prove ourselves to God; we study to prove to ourselves that we're already approved by God! He explains:

The Word is a love letter. The purpose of the Bible is to communicate God's love. The Word does give us a standard of morality, but this is not its main purpose. The Bible also teaches us right from wrong, but again that is not the main goal. The aim of the Word of God is to show you that you have a Father who loves you very much.

If you study the Word for any other reason, you will not be able to rightly divide the Word of Truth. That is a radical statement. . . . Every time you open your Bible, your heart's intent should be, "Father, show me how much You love me. I open my heart to believe the truth about how much You accept me. Reveal to me in a deeper way what was accomplished and achieved on my behalf. Let this be firmly established in my heart."[20]

That's the way I want to read the Bible. That's the way I want to study the Bible. That's the way I want to preach the Bible . . . because that's the way God intended us to absorb it.

HYPER-LAW

Old Testament, New Testament—the delineation is right there in our Bibles. We assume that the new covenant starts with Matthew 1:1, but it doesn't. As we've seen, it begins near the end of each of the Gospels as Jesus breathed His last breath on the cross. Before that, we see Him as the Messiah born under the law, in a culture that was wedded to the law, among leaders who added to the law, and with people who feared the condemnation of the law. Since the first century, people have been amazed at Jesus' teaching, and the most famous of His messages is the Sermon on the Mount. People often say things like: "Isn't it a wonderful sermon;" "It gives us such a positive way to live;" "I think everybody should live like this." But such responses just show that those people either have never read it, haven't understood it, or have never taken it seriously.

I used to tell people, "You need to stick to the red letter sections in your Bibles. Those are the very words of Jesus." Yes, they are, but they may not say what you think they say. Jesus took the law (that no one could fully obey) and raised the bar to new heights. For instance, take a closer look at some of the things He told them.

- "You have heard that it was said to the people long ago, 'You shall not murder, and anyone who murders will be subject to judgment.' But I tell you that anyone who is angry with a brother or sister will be subject to judgment" (Matthew 5:21-22).

- But He wasn't finished with fresh demands: "Again, anyone who says to a brother or sister, 'Raca,' is answerable to the court. And anyone who says, 'You fool!' will be in danger of the fire of hell" (v. 22).

- "You have heard that it was said, 'You shall not commit adultery.' But I tell you that anyone who looks at a woman lustfully has already committed adultery with her in his heart" (vv. 27-28).

- "Again, you have heard that it was said to the people long ago, 'Do not break your oath, but fulfill to the Lord the vows you have made.' But I tell you, do not swear an oath at all: either by heaven, for it is God's throne; or by the earth, for it is his footstool; or by Jerusalem, for it is the city of the Great King. And do not swear by your head, for you cannot make even one hair white or black. All you need to say is simply 'Yes' or 'No'; anything beyond this comes from the evil one" (vv. 33-37).

- In a time when people felt oppressed by the Roman occupying forces, this one would have been hard to hear: "You have heard that it was said, 'Eye for eye, and tooth for tooth.' But I tell you, do not resist an evil person. If anyone slaps you on the right cheek, turn to them the other cheek also. And if anyone wants to sue you and take your shirt, hand over your coat as well. If anyone forces you to go one mile, go with them two miles. Give to the one who asks you, and do not turn away from the one who wants to borrow from you" (vv. 38-42).

- And to raise the bar through the roof, He told them, "If your right eye causes you to stumble, gouge it out and throw it away. It is better for you to lose one part of your body than for your whole body to be thrown into hell. And if your right hand causes you to stumble, cut it off and throw it away. It is better for you to lose one part of your body than for your whole body to go into hell" (vv. 29-30).

Years ago, college professor Virginia Stem Owens assigned the Sermon on the Mount to her freshman class and asked them to write a report. Texas A&M is a prestigious university, with students largely from conservative families. She expected them to be familiar with the text and "express a modicum of piety" in their responses. What she read surprised her. The comments included:

- "I did not like the essay 'Sermon the Mount.' It was hard to read and made me feel like I had to be perfect and no one is."

- "The stuff the churches preach is extremely strict and allows for almost no fun without thinking it is a sin or not."

- "The things asked in this sermon are absurd. To look at a woman is adultery? That is the most extreme, stupid, un-human statement that I have ever heard."

The students were reading the sermon without a predetermined idea of what they'd find, and what they found offended them. Owens concludes: "At this point I began to be encouraged. There is something exquisitely innocent about not realizing you shouldn't call Jesus stupid. . . . This was the real thing, a pristine response to the gospel, unfiltered through a two-millennia cultural haze."[21]

I'd disagree with Professor Owens on one point: She assumed Jesus was preaching the gospel in His most famous sermon, but He was preaching the law to show people how much they fall short of God's standards. Still, the response of the students is strangely refreshing.

They understood the demands of the law! I'm certainly not suggesting
we should call Jesus stupid, but I recommend we take the blinders off
and really look at the sermon. It's not a set of really nice sentiments;
it's a standard of life none of us can meet. Was Jesus being harsh? No,
He was showing in no uncertain terms that "all fall short of the glory
of God." But the cross opened the door to a new way to relate to God.
Jesus didn't abolish the law; He fulfilled it . . . perfectly. In fact, He fulfilled it in two ways: He lived a perfect life (which is credited to us), and
He paid the full penalty for sin (which is also credited to our account).
Laws are fulfilled if people follow them, or they are fulfilled if people
pay the fine when they break them. Jesus did both for us.

> **It's not a set of really nice sentiments;
> it's a standard of life none of us can meet.
> Was Jesus being harsh? No, He was
> showing in no uncertain terms that
> "all fall short of the glory of God."**

I used to misinterpret the Sermon on the Mount much as I did
Paul's encouragement to Timothy to study to show yourself approved.
I told people that obeying Jesus' commands in the sermon proved
their loyalty to Him. I was heaping law on them, and for that, I ask for
forgiveness.

Does this mean I don't value Christ's teaching in the Gospels? Am
I recommending we ignore everything in them up to the Passion of
Jesus? No way! Everything He said was exactly, completely true, right,
and good, but His standards of obedience are pure law showing us

that we're hopeless apart from His grace. In fact, every word He uttered magnified grace.

For far too long, I tried to blend and balance law and grace, but they aren't meant to be balanced; they're meant to be sequential—law comes before grace to show our need for it. Religion makes us stupid. For a long time, I misunderstood a popular passage in John's Revelation: "To the angel of the church of Laodicea write: These are the words of the Amen, the faithful and true witness, the ruler of God's creation. I know your deeds, that you are neither cold nor hot. I wish you were either one or the other! So, because you are lukewarm—neither hot nor cold—I am about to spit you out of my mouth" (Revelation 3:14-16). I assumed hot and cold referred to passion, so I believed God was saying, "Ben, you've got to get hot for Jesus! You need to be amped up for Him!" I tried my best to feel passionate about Christ. Do you know what happens when we try to manufacture feelings? They may be enflamed for a short while, but sooner or later they leave us feeling flat. When that happened to me, I was sure something was very wrong with me, so I tried even harder to feel the passion . . . and the confusing, destructive cycle continued.

The passage about not being lukewarm isn't about passion; it's about covenants. The law is stone-cold condemnation because we can't measure up, but grace is the white-hot love of God poured into us like molten gold! If you try to blend law and grace, you get two things: mental confusion and lukewarm emotions. Real, authentic passion isn't something we generate to prove we're sold out to God. When we embrace grace, we don't even have to think about our emotions. We discover they're appropriate for every situation: gratitude or sorrow, righteous anger or praise, peace, and joy.

I've heard pastors say, "The Bible says it. I believe it. that settles it." And I've seen others slap their Bibles and proclaim, "I believe everything in this book from leather to leather! If it's in the Bible, we need to obey it." (This line doesn't make much sense these days when we have the Scriptures on our smartphones!)

Okay, Pastor, what about the severe punishments in the Old Testament? Are you going to stone the person in your church who has committed adultery (Leviticus 20:10) . . . or anyone carrying firewood on the Sabbath (Numbers 15:32-36)? Will you line up all the kids in your youth group and execute those who have dishonored their parents (Exodus 21:15, 17)? The list could go on. And will you heed Jesus' New Testament command to cut off your own hand and gouge out your eye when you sin? No, I didn't think so.

Surely, most of the dramatic declarations by these pastors are taken with a grain of salt, but for some people in their congregations, the pastor's passionate words add to their load of guilt and shame. How many people suffer from chronic anxiety at least partly because they hear far more law than grace? How many are depressed? How many feel isolated because they don't feel worthy of love from God or anyone else? And how many have thought about taking their own lives because they've internalized the unreachable requirements of the law and have missed the wonder of grace? I'm not putting this burden only on pastors. Some people have been wounded in other relationships, and they don't have the ability to sort through their pastor's words and the Bible's clear teaching about grace. But to be honest, I didn't either.

THE LENS OF GRACE

We need Jesus to be our optometrist. We need a new set of lenses to read the Bible more accurately and see every aspect of our lives from His perspective. Without these new glasses, we can't rightly divide law from grace . . . it all looks like a blurry mess. For instance, we shouldn't be surprised when we read that Paul reminded Timothy, "We also know that the law is made not for the righteous but for the lawbreakers" (1 Timothy 1:9), because, as we've seen, the law reveals unrighteousness and the need to repent. The righteous—that is, those who have been credited with Christ's own righteousness—are indwelt by the Spirit of God, and He is making us more like Jesus. The fruit of the Spirit is being formed in us, and "against such things there is no law" (Galatians 5:23).

I don't have to go to the county courthouse to study laws on child abuse to know how to treat my son and my daughter. The laws aren't my guide or my deterrent. I love my children, and the fruit of the Spirit is being borne out in me so that I spontaneously and joyfully love them!

As we've noted, many Christians see salvation only as a ticket to heaven, and they're convinced they live under the law all day every day until they die and go to be with Jesus. They're missing out on the joy, freedom, and love He offers us now! We don't need to struggle to earn God's love. We already have it! We don't need to worry about being accepted by God. We can't be more accepted than we are now! We don't have to labor to try to be closer to God. We can't be any closer than being in Christ! We don't need to beg God to do what He's already done or give us what He's already graciously given.

They're missing out on the joy, freedom, and love He offers us now! We don't need to struggle to earn God's love. We already have it!

Do you struggle with guilt and shame? That's a product of law, not grace.

Do you feel like you never measure up? That's looking at life through the lens of law, not grace.

In your Bible reading and prayer time, do you feel more aware of your failures than God's tender affection for you? That's the effect of the law, not grace.

Have you given up because you've tried so hard and you've failed so miserably? You've met law face to face, and law crushed you.

It's time to rightly divide the Word of truth, separate law from grace, and camp out in the matchless, unlimited, unmerited love of God.

Law makes you conclude you're unloved and unlovable, ashamed and beyond hope, grasping but not getting, and an orphan instead of a son or daughter. That's life in the jungle. But the moment you fix your heart on the wonder of God's grace, you come out of the jungle. The fresh breeze of His love feels so good. You feel adored, free, supplied with everything you could want, and embraced by your Father.

STARK CONTRASTS

Even though as believers we're not under law but under grace, we still suffer the effects of our old life under the law because it's so deeply imprinted on our minds. That's a law mindset, which causes us to rely on our performance to be acceptable. People with a law mindset try to earn what God has already given.

When I teach these truths in our Gospel Circles or The Gospel Institute, I give participants a handout of "101 Simple Comparisons Between Law & Grace." I want to include a few of the comparisons and contrasts here. Don't rush past them. They're important:

Law Mindset (Old Covenant)	Grace Mindset (New Covenant)
God's people are worried about "sin in the camp."	We rejoice that Jesus has forgiven us of all sin.
God's people are slaves to sin.	We're slaves to righteousness.
The Holy Spirit convicts people of sin.	The Spirit convicts people of Christ's righteousness that has been credited to us.
The focus is on self-sacrifice and good works.	The focus is on the sacrifice and finished work of Jesus.
God's people fight for victory.	We fight with confidence because the victory is already won.
God's people ask for forgiveness.	We're assured that we're already forgiven.
God's people try to get closer to God.	We're already in union with Him, and we can't get any closer.
God's people plead for a breakthrough.	God has already broken through in Jesus.
God's people hope to someday go to heaven.	We're already seated with Christ in heaven at the right hand of the Father.
God's people are compelled to manage their image.	Our identity in Christ is secure.

Law Mindset (Old Covenant)	Grace Mindset (New Covenant)
God's people ask, "What Would Jesus Do?"	We say, "Watch What Jesus Does!"
God's people serve because they have to.	We serve because we want to, out of gratitude.
God's people are well aware of their flaws.	We're thrilled that Christ's death is credited to us for forgiveness and His perfect life is credited to us for righteousness.
God's people are obsessed with the need to obey.	We're thrilled that Jesus obeyed and has qualified us to share in His inheritance.

This is just a sample of the contrasts between trying to earn God's love by obeying the law and knowing we're loved by God because of grace. When a person is introduced to the differences, it may be difficult to detect the distinctions between law and grace in sermons, books, podcasts, and conversations. To make it clear, you can ask a simple question: "Does this teaching or practice point to Christ and His performance on our behalf, or does it teach that God's love is conditional and is based on our performance?"

If it points to Christ and celebrates what He has done for you, it's grace.

If it puts the burden on what you've done or what you must do, it's law.

In other words, grace makes you Christ-conscious, and law makes you self-conscious.

DECLARATION:

From now on, I'll rightly divide law and grace.

CONSIDER THIS:

1. What are some problems that arise when we don't rightly divide law and grace when we read the Bible?

2. What are some benefits when we do?

3. Does it shock you, amuse you, or encourage you that I said Jesus' teaching before the cross is "hyper-law"? Explain your answer.

4. Carefully read the comparisons between law and grace at the end of the chapter, and circle the ones that are most meaningful to you. What do you find enlightening or encouraging in these statements?

5. Write a paragraph or two of what the concepts in this chapter mean to you.

CHAPTER 9

AFTER THE *BUT*

SEEN VS. UNSEEN

FOR MANY YEARS, MY FOCUS WAS ON THE PAST AND THE FUTURE, not the present. I could look at the past and believe that Jesus died for my sins, and I looked to the future and believed I'd be in heaven with Him someday, but I didn't understand how God could bring spiritual truth and power into my life all day every day. I was convinced (though I don't think I ever actually said it to anyone as clearly as this) that I was pretty much on my own to live the Christian life, and I needed to try harder because I wasn't doing such a great job at it!

We're visceral people. We eat, drink, play, hug, work, write, sleep, and do all the other things that make life work, but far too often, we stop there. Our eyes are fixed on the tangible, and we aren't aware of the intangible world all around us. Paul was a realist, but his reality wasn't limited to the five senses. In his second letter to the Corinthians, he explained the supernatural nature of his calling, and he also explained the supernatural nature of spiritual life for all of us. He identified with the hardships we experience, but he injected hope that God would still reign in each difficulty: "But we have this treasure in jars of clay to show that this all-surpassing power is from God and not from us" (2 Corinthians 4:7).

Paul followed his own advice to "set your minds on things above" when he pulled back the curtain to show the Corinthians what's really going on in their lives: "Therefore we do not lose heart. Though outwardly we are wasting away, yet inwardly we are being renewed day by day. For our light and momentary troubles are achieving for us an eternal glory that far outweighs them all. So we fix our eyes not on what is seen, but on what is unseen, since what is seen is temporary, but what is unseen is eternal" (vv. 16-18).

How in the world do you fix your eyes on what is unseen? With spiritual perception. When we lack this sight, the word "but" always has a negative connotation. In *The Rest of the Gospel*, Dan Stone and David Gregory observe, "People always live after the but. The word, I mean: *but*. Go out and listen to people talk. Everyone lives after the but, whether they're Christians or not. I don't care what they say first, before the but. It's after the but that you hear what they really believe."[22]

They offer several illustrations, but let me adapt some of them:

"I like Pastor Ben, but his sermons are dry."

"I know God loves me, but it sure doesn't seem like it."

"God promised to provide, but it seems He has forgotten me."

"The Bible promises wisdom if we ask, but I've asked and I'm still confused."

"We need to love our enemies, but people on the other side of the political world are stupid and evil."

Some believers try to remedy the disparity between the seen and the unseen by denying the seen. I've heard people say, "Pastor Ben, I'm just claiming the doctor will change his mind about the diagnosis. I'm claiming I don't have cancer!" They don't want to face the reality of a disease, a wayward child, a debt, a fading memory, or any other very real problem people may face. Paul didn't live in a fantasy world. He was painfully honest about the reality of suffering, setbacks, and opposition, but he brought the unseen reality of the gospel into the seen reality of his troubles.

THE OTHER SIDE OF *BUT*

Those who have a grasp of the unseen world also use the word *but*, yet it has the opposite effect. They see the realities of the world around them, and then they trust the God they can't see to work His will and ways in what they see. I've heard them say:

"My son is very sick, but I believe that by His stripes, he'll be healed."

"I lost my job, but I'm sure God has something even better for me."

"My daughter has been doing drugs, but God is willing to use anything for good."

"Our country is going in the wrong direction, but Christ in me will help me make a difference in the people around me."

Jesus demonstrated living with a holy *but*. When He was misunderstood and pressured to provide even more bread for those who had been at the outdoor feast, He told them, "For I have come down from heaven not to do my will but to do the will of him who sent me" (John 6:38). And at the moment of His most severe trial in the Garden of Gethsemane, Jesus pleaded with the Father to rescue Him out of the torture He faced. In this case, the translators used *yet* instead of *but*: "*Abba*, Father, everything is possible for you. Take this cup from me. Yet not what I will, but what you will" (Mark 14:36).

Paul followed Jesus' example. In his letter to the Corinthians when he said we're "jars of clay," he then added a series of *buts* to remind us that what we see isn't the end of the story . . . and it isn't the whole story: "We are hard pressed on every side, but not crushed; perplexed, but not in despair; persecuted, but not abandoned; struck down, but not destroyed" (2 Corinthians 4:8-9). Paul then ties the concept of our being dead in Christ to this robust certainty that God is at work in us and through us even when we can't see it: " We always carry around in our body the death of Jesus, so that the life of Jesus may also be revealed in our body. For we who are alive are always being given over to death for Jesus' sake, so that his life may also be revealed in our mortal body" (vs. 10-11).

A mark of growing in grace is the ability to see ourselves, our situations, and other people through spiritual eyes, to see the unseen, to grasp the intangible, to fix our minds on things above.

A mark of growing in grace is the ability to see ourselves, our situations, and other people through spiritual eyes, to see the unseen, to grasp the intangible, to fix our minds on things above. This doesn't make us lose touch with the world. Not in the least. In fact, it enables us to be more honest about the struggles we face because we aren't as threatened by what we can see around us. The writer to the Hebrews encouraged us to look at life from God's perspective. When we feel hopeless, helpless, confused, or alone, we need to raise our eyes to see Jesus:

> Therefore, since we have a great high priest who has ascended into heaven, Jesus the Son of God, let us hold firmly to the faith we profess. For we do not have a high priest who is unable to empathize with our weaknesses, but we have one who has been tempted in every way, just as we are—yet he did not sin. Let us then approach God's throne of grace with confidence, so that we may receive mercy and find grace to help us in our time of need. (Hebrews 4:14-16)

Many of us are guided far more by our emotions than God's truth in the unseen world, and our circumstances dictate what we feel at any given moment. We worry that God won't come through. We're anxious about what people will think of us. We're angry that our hopes have been dashed. We're afraid that we won't have enough. We're terrified that we'll be alone. All of these perspectives put the *but* in the wrong place.

Let me go back to the points in this book to illustrate the importance of having the *but* in the right place. For too long, we've lived this way:

> "The Bible says God loves me, but I feel so unlovable."

> "I want to measure up to please God, but no matter how hard I try, it's never enough."

"I try so hard to squeeze every bit of meaning out of life, but I still feel empty."

"I want to feel close to God, but it feels like He's a million miles away."

"I'm haunted with guilt, but I guess I just need to try harder."

"We sing in church about victory, but I feel like a victim."

There's another script based on gospel truth:

"Sometimes I don't feel lovable, but Jesus has proved His great love for me!"

"The enemy lies and tries to get me to try harder, but Jesus has done it all for me!"

"I feel so much inner conflict, but thank God, I'm dead to my old life!"

"My past hurts and sins sometimes make me feel distant from God, but Jesus lives in me!"

"I occasionally feel too dirty to go to God, but He has credited me with Jesus' death and righteousness!"

"Self-pity still rears its ugly head and I feel sorry for myself, but I'm not an orphan!"

In several places in the Psalms, the writer specifically talks to himself . . . which is exactly what we need to do sometimes. For instance, in Psalm 42, the psalmist is deeply discouraged. He compares his spiritual condition to a deer dying of thirst. Twice the writer says,

Why, my soul, are you downcast?

Why so disturbed within me?

Put your hope in God,

for I will yet praise him,

my Savior and my God. (Psalm 42:5, 11)

His self-talk redirects his heart so he can focus on God's power and love instead of his current predicament. In effect, he was saying to himself, "I feel empty and alone, but God still reigns. I feel desolate, but God hasn't forgotten me. Other people laugh at me, but God delights in me. I'm in physical pain, but God has supplied everything I need!" If he had listened only to his painful emotions, he would have continued to spiral down into despair. Instead, he talked to his soul like a wise and trusted friend would talk to him, encouraging him, strengthening him, and giving him God's perspective. If the psalmist was able to do this before the cross, just think how much more we can do it after the cross! Our emotions can dictate where we put the *but*, and we have the opportunity to rewrite our sentences by speaking authoritatively to our souls.

> **Instead, he talked to his soul like a wise and trusted friend would talk to him, encouraging him, strengthening him, and giving him God's perspective.**

I don't think it's off-base to say that where we put the *but* shows whether we are applying the truths of the gospel or not. When we're unsure of who we are in Christ, fear and doubt cloud our minds and undermine our faith. We wonder if we're safe in God's hands, we wonder if

He'll really come through like He promised, we're afraid we'll be swept away by the difficulties we face, and we think we'll be crushed under the unrelenting pressures. But as we embrace the gospel truth that we're in Christ, we increasingly live with the joy and freedom that come from our understanding that all our sins have been paid for—not by our guilt and penance, but by the blood of Jesus. And we've been imparted with the very righteousness of Christ, so when God looks at us, He sees the purity of Jesus in us.

If that doesn't give you a beautiful blend of relief and joy, I wonder if you still have a pulse!

TWO VIEWS

Some people might respond, "That's absurd! We have to see things as they really are." And I'd answer, "Precisely." There are *really* two worlds, two realities, two views. When we see things as they really are, we live as if both are true . . . because both *are* absolutely true. The Corinthians thought they were pretty sharp, and in fact, they thought they had it all figured out. Paul told them, "Do not deceive yourselves. If any of you think you are wise by the standards of this age, you should become 'fools' so that you may become wise. For the wisdom of this world is foolishness in God's sight. As it is written: 'He catches the wise in their craftiness'" (1 Corinthians 3:18-19).

Are you holding both realities, the seen and the unseen, in your mind and heart? Most of us wouldn't deny the unseen world, but we ignore it. The consequences are the same. We're left trying to make life work on our own terms, guided by our own logic, and buffeted by circumstances and our fickle feelings.

Many who are reading this are thinking, *Pastor Ben, I already know the truths about the gospel. You've helped clarify some things, but I'm a believer, so I'm not sure how all this applies to me.* My point is that we can know the truths backward and forward, but if we put them on the wrong side of the *but*, we're actually living only in the seen world instead of both worlds. The enemy of our souls understands all the doctrines, and he's happy for us to study them, recite them, and teach them . . . as long as we keep them on the wrong side of the *but*. When we say, "Yes, I'm totally forgiven and declared righteous because the death and life of Jesus have been credited to me, but I'm still a loser," the enemy is having his way with us.

Faith is much more than a feeling. Feelings are fine . . . as long as we don't trust in them to tell us what's real. They're the flashing light on the dashboard of our lives to show us what's going on inside, but they're not the engine. I love the passage in Hebrews 11 about the heroes of the faith. They weren't heroes because they didn't have problems; they were heroes because they had the necessary double perspective, so they trusted God even when things looked bleak. The writer gives a brief synopsis of the lives of Noah, Abraham, Isaac, Jacob, Joseph, Moses, and others, and he explains:

All these people were still living by faith when they died. They did not receive the things promised; they only saw them and welcomed them from a distance, admitting that they were foreigners and strangers on earth. People who say such things show that they are looking for a country of their own. If they had been thinking of the country they had left, they would have had opportunity to return. Instead, they were longing for a better country—a heavenly one. Therefore God is not ashamed to be called their God, for he has prepared a city for them. (Hebrews 11:13-16)

In His great prayer on the night He was betrayed, Jesus asked the Father to enable us to be in the world, but not of the world (John 17:16). In other words, we have dual citizenship. That's what the writer to the Hebrews was talking about in the chapter on faithful believers in the Old Testament. These men and women were very much aware of the struggles they faced, but they were "looking for a country of their own," "a better country—a heavenly one." But don't miss this: their hope wasn't just empty air. The great God of the universe "has prepared a city for them." Their hope in the unseen realities were based on the solid foundation of God's promises.

OTHER *BUTS*

If we pay attention as we read the Scriptures, we'll find *buts* all through the pages. We could look at dozens of examples, but let me point out just a few. (I've added the italics in each case.)

- After their father Jacob died, Joseph's brothers were afraid that he'd take revenge on them for selling him into slavery many years before. Joseph identified the two realities, the seen and the unseen: "But Joseph said to them, 'Don't be afraid. Am I in the place of God? You intended to harm me, *but God* intended it for good to accomplish what is now being done, the saving of many lives. So then, don't be afraid. I will provide for you and your children.' And he reassured them and spoke kindly to them" (Genesis 50:19-21).

- David had already been anointed the next king of Israel, but Saul hadn't yet given up his throne. Instead, Saul and his army chased David and his few followers around the countryside, trying to kill them. The historian tells us, "David stayed in the desert strongholds and in the hills of the Desert of Ziph. Day after day Saul searched for him, *but God* did not give David into his hands" (1 Samuel 23:14).

- In one of the most threatening moments in Israel's history, a mighty army camped just outside Jerusalem, preparing to wipe them off the map. The prophet encouraged the people to look at both realities: "Listen, King Jehoshaphat and all who live in Judah and Jerusalem! This is what the Lord says to you: 'Do not be afraid or discouraged because of this vast army. For the battle is not yours, *but God's'*" (2 Chronicles 20:15).

- Jesus continually revealed the love and power that exists in the God-drenched unseen world. When His followers didn't understand some of His comments about obstacles to entering the kingdom of God and questioned how anyone could be saved, He told them, "With man this is impossible, *but with God* all things are possible" (Matthew 19:26).

- A passage we're all familiar with is in Paul's letter to the Romans: "For the wages of sin is death, *but the gift of God* is eternal life in Christ Jesus our Lord" (Romans 6:23).

- And the one that perhaps is most dear to me is in Paul's letter to the Ephesians. He vividly describes our hopelessness apart from God, and then he describes God's intervention: "And you were dead in your trespasses and sins. . . . and were by nature children of wrath, like the rest of mankind. *But God,* being rich in mercy, because of the great love with which he loved us, even when we were dead in our trespasses, made us alive together with Christ—by grace you have been saved" (Ephesians 2:1, 3-5 ESV).

As you read and study, look for the *buts*. You'll find a lot of them, and they'll remind you to live on the right side of them.

A BIG DIFFERENCE

Does being on the right side of the *but* really make a difference? You bet it does! Let me give a few examples.

- Janice and Rob are having trouble with their teenage daughter. Sarah was caught at school smoking marijuana in the bathroom, and when they tried to talk to her about it, she blew up at them: "You don't get it, do you? Everybody smokes, and I'm sure you did too when you were my age! Leave me alone!"

  In the past when they had confrontations with their kids, Janice cratered and became passive, and Rob got furious and tried to control every aspect of their lives. Now, they're learning to live in the new covenant of grace, with more hope and power than they ever dreamed possible. This time, when they confronted Sarah about her offense at school, their reactions were very different than in the past. Janice didn't melt into the floor in self-condemnation and shame. Instead, she stood upright, looked her daughter in the eyes, and with a combination of compassion and strength told her, "Honey, let's talk about what happened. I want to understand, but you need to know that this isn't acceptable. I want to hear your solutions."

  Sarah was waiting for her father to lower the boom like he always did, but this time, he didn't seem fierce and furious. And he wasn't out of control, demanding compliance without listening to a word she said. No, this time was different. He took a few breaths, remembered the forgiveness he had experienced through Christ, and joined Janice by saying, "Yes,

Sarah. We want to know more of what you're thinking. And we want you to tell us what you think needs to happen about your smoking. Together, we'll figure this out."

As the couple learned how to live in the gospel, Sarah didn't magically change. In fact, she was caught a couple of other times and was suspended for a month—but Janice and Rob changed. They were honest about the situation, and they learned to see the unseen: God is greater than Sarah's disobedience and rebellion, God is wiser than they are, and God will accomplish His purposes one way or another.

- A lady in our church had been feeling fatigued for several months, and she finally went to the doctor. When the test results came back, the doctor called her in for a consultation. It wasn't a good sign that he didn't give her the news on the phone. She was correct in her suspicions: he told her she had stage 4 pancreatic cancer.

  Over the next several days as the treatment plan was developed, friends tried to console her, but instead, she encouraged them. She told each one, "Yes, I have a really bad form of cancer, and the doctors say it's terminal. But I have a life that will never end. I'm just beginning to live!" Her eyes were on the magnificent hope in the unseen world instead of the dismal projections set before her. She was already living in another world.

- José lost his job due to the pandemic. He filed for unemployment, but it took the state several weeks to process his claim. He looked for another job every day, but nothing opened up. His wife had just had their third child, and all the kids were under six years old. The financial strain was severe. He didn't know how he was going to keep a roof over their heads and buy enough food for his young and growing family.

Some friends from his former job came to his house. They had two reasons for their visit: they wanted to know if he'd found a job and if there were any other openings, and they wanted to complain about how unfair things were. Their self-pity and rage spilled out like a dam had burst. José listened, but then he told them, "Yes, things are pretty bad, but God is still in control. I'm not sure where the money will come from, but God will provide. He always does. I sometimes feel sorry for myself, but there's no need for that because I know that God has a plan, a good plan, for me and my family."

Much of the discourse in our country today is myopic—totally fixed on the seen world and completely missing God's perspective. And it's not just the secular media that's so near-sighted. Many Christians communicate just as much venom, just as much self-pity, just as much of a victim mentality, and just as much self-righteousness as unbelievers. And again, I'm not suggesting that everything is fine and we need to just shut up. There are real problems, real injustices, and real needs, but there's also a real unseen world of God's infinite love, forgiveness, purpose, wisdom, and power. Do you hear Christians talk about that very often? No, me either.

There are real problems, real injustices, and real needs, but there's also a real unseen world of God's infinite love, forgiveness, purpose, wisdom, and power.

Disease, death, unemployment, and heartaches of all kinds are stark realities, but that's never the whole story. If God could be at work during His people's slavery in Egypt, the Babylonian exile, and the Roman occupation of their land, we can be confident He's present and powerful in every aspect of our lives today, even if we don't see His hand at work.

What are you hearing from believers? What side of the *but* are they living on?

What's coming out of your mouth? What does the placement of your *but* say about your eyesight?

Our five senses don't have the last word—and if we're smart, they don't even have the first word! Beyond our senses is a very real world where spiritual battles are fought, God's angels are active to protect and provide, and God is weaving His will into the seen world like a beautiful tapestry. We only see a few threads or get a glimpse of the back of it, but it's there. Count on it.

DECLARATION:

But God _____.

(Fill in the blank with your current concerns.)

CONSIDER THIS:

1. Describe what you think it means to have a "dual citizenship," to be "in the world but not of the world."

2. What are some examples you think of when you identify statements with *but* on the wrong side?

3. Think of one or two situations you're in right now. What is a statement about each one with *but* on the right side?

4. Does believing in the reality of the unseen world make us more or less objective about the problems in our lives? Explain your answer.

5. What difference will it make for you to develop the habit of living after the *but*?

CHAPTER 10

EMPOWERING GRACE

LEGAL VS. VITAL

WE'VE ALL HEARD THE OLD ADAGE, "LIFE'S A JOURNEY, NOT A destination," however, when we're young we may not realize the accuracy of this statement. When I was a boy and our family was on a road trip, I was like most kids and incessantly asked, "Dad, how much longer before we get there?"

Just as predictably, he looked over his shoulder and told me, "Son, we're five minutes closer than the last time you asked."

A few years later, I came to that point every teenager has circled on a mental calendar: high school graduation. For four years, I anticipated the day I'd wear a robe and walk on stage to receive my diploma, but as the day approached, my dad again had a valuable insight for me: "Ben, we're so proud of you and all you've accomplished. Your graduation is one of the biggest days of your life, but here's the truth: It's just the beginning, not the end. That's why they call it a *commencement*. It's the start of a new adventure in your life."

Many believers need to hear my dad's wisdom and take it to heart—not about high school graduation, but about their spiritual lives. The day they receive Christ, they celebrate the relief and joy of the moment, but too often, it's like a sign flashes: "Mission accomplished!" They believe they've attained the ultimate spiritual prize. In one way, they're right: at that moment, they experience the forgiveness won by Christ on the cross, and they've been given everything they need for life and godliness. Yet this moment is much like a high school graduation commencement service—it's a beginning, not an end. Jesus said that coming to know Him is the beginning of "the abundant life," not "the last stop on the trip."

Grace was powerfully at work the day you were saved, but there's another aspect of grace that empowers us all day every day. The *legal* aspect of grace is the verdict that the payment has been made, the cell door has been opened, we're forgiven and free! The *vital* nature of grace is the power to walk with God and fulfill the destiny He gives each of us. We often sing of the wonder of the legal part of grace: "Amazing grace, how sweet the sound, that saved a wretch like me." And thank God, it's true! But grace didn't end at that moment. God's unmerited grace saved you, and His unlimited grace empowers you to live a truly abundant life.

We need to grasp the fact that legal grace saves us and vital grace empowers us. To make it clearer:

- Saving grace carried you, but you carry empowering grace in every activity in your life.

- Saving grace was done for you, but empowering grace is God's power in you and through you.

- Saving grace operates vertically, from heaven to earth, but empowering grace operates horizontally, from you to others.

Jesus is the author and perfecter of our faith (Hebrews 12:2), which means you were saved by His grace and you're kept by His grace. He began a good work in you, and He will complete it (Philippians 1:6).

All Christians understand they were saved *from* something, but many don't realize they're saved *for* something.

All Christians understand they were saved from something, but many don't realize they're saved for something. With this limited grasp of spiritual reality, they're just biding time in the backseat waiting to get to heaven. God's purpose isn't just to get us to heaven. The gospel tells us that God wants to use us to bring heaven to earth. In Jesus' model prayer, He told us to pray, "Your kingdom come, your will be done, on earth as it is in heaven" (Matthew 6:10). God's purpose and our destiny isn't just to get us from here to there, but to bring the power, love, and wisdom of there to here.

The "something" you're saved for is your divine calling . . . a calling specifically designed by God for you . . . a calling that only you can fulfill. To fulfill this calling, we have to grow up spiritually and know God's grace in both dimensions—legal and vital, saving grace and empowering grace. God has "brought us out" of darkness to "bring us in" to His glorious light. As we've seen, we've been *purchased* by Jesus, our high priest, and we've been *purposed* by Jesus, our sovereign King.

A CHILD AND A SON

The two words, *child* and *son*, may seem synonymous, but in the Scriptures, they have significantly different meanings. In Paul's letter to the Romans, we see the difference: "The Spirit himself bears witness with our spirit that we are children of God" (Romans 8:16), but "For as many as are led by the Spirit of God, these are sons of God (Romans 8:14 NKJV). As adopted *children* of God, we have a secure relationship with Him, but the term *son* signifies maturity in the relationship, and sons display the character, personality, and heart of their Father. Paul wrote, "For the earnest expectation of the creation eagerly waits for the revealing of the sons of God" (Romans 8:19 NKJV).

(As we saw in the first chapter, men shouldn't take offense at being called "the bride of Christ"! In this case, ladies, please don't be offended by being called "sons." In fact, since sons received an inheritance and daughters didn't in ancient times, Paul is making the revolutionary statement that men and women are equal in the eyes of God. [See Galatians 3:26-29.])

Let's look at the way children and sons are described in Paul's letters. First, children:

- A child is immature. (1 Corinthians 3:1)

- A child is incapable of handling an inheritance. (Galatians 4:1)

- A child is led by senses (elements of the world). (Galatians 4:3)

- A child is still in bondage. (Galatians 4:3)

- A child must be cared for. (Galatians 4:2)

- A child who is an heir is the owner of everything, but he acts like a slave. (Galatians 4:1)

- A child is kept under guardians. (Galatians 4:1)

But the role of sons is much different. The Gospels and Paul help us understand:

- A son is grown and mature. (Romans 8:14)
- A son is the master of all things given by the Father. (John 17:10)
- A son cares for others. (John 6:38)
- A son doesn't need a guardian. (Galatians 4:2-5)
- A son possesses all things. (Galatians 4:7)
- A son is led by the Spirit and his Father's will. (Romans 8:14)

Or, to put it succinctly:

- A child is still a slave, but a son is a prince.
- A child is bound, but a son is free.
- A child is a burden, but a son is a burden-bearer.
- A child is a liability, but a son is an asset.
- A child consumes, but a son contributes.

Of course, the stage of being a child is perfectly good, right, and normal . . . for a while. Paul explained to the Corinthians, who were acting very childishly in their jealousy and pettiness, "When I was a child, I talked like a child, I thought like a child, I reasoned like a child. When I became a man, I put the ways of childhood behind me" (1 Corinthians 13:11).

It may be surprising to read that a Christian who is still a child remains in bondage. Actually, freedom has already been granted, but immature believers often act like they're still slaves of sin. They careen between law and grace, one moment certain God can only love them if they obey with all their hearts, and the next basking in the joy of His grace . . . and then back again. They haven't yet made the distinction between legalism (following rules to be accepted), moralism (trying to be a good enough person for God to accept them), and grace (the reality that God accepts them only because of Christ's sacrifice). Legalism and moralism are rampant in our churches. We can sing songs of grace but walk away hearing only that we need to try harder to be accepted by God . . . and if we try harder than other people, we're better than them!

Religion makes slaves; the gospel makes sons.

Religion tells you what's wrong with you; the gospel assures you that Jesus has made you right with God.

Religion focuses on what you aren't; the gospel proclaims who you are in Christ.

Religion condemns you; the gospel affirms you.

Religion is an attempt to shape up your old way of life; the gospel is based on the love and power of your new identity.

When believers only know what they've been saved *from* but not saved *for*, they live on a spiritual rollercoaster . . . and the ride is exhausting and confusing. They need to understand that empowering grace gives them the direction, heart, and power to fulfill their God-given kingdom assignment here and now.

HAUNTS AND DAYDREAMS

For far too many of us, our thoughts are consumed with the past or the future—past sins and hurts that haunt us, or daydreams that promise a future escape from our problems. But God's grace enables us to live *right now*, to grasp the wonder that we're redeemed from the past and our future is secure. We can devote our energies to live for God today by the leading and power of the Holy Spirit.

When I've spoken on our new identity in Christ, some people have come up to me after my message with their eyes cast down. They say, "Pastor, you don't understand. I'm divorced. God can't use me because I'm so flawed." Or "I've just gotten out of prison. I've done some horrible things." Or "I think God has given up on me because I can't get over a recurring bad habit. It's eating my lunch!" These statements—and dozens like them that are spoken or unspoken—are lies from the pit of hell.

These statements—and dozens like them that are spoken or unspoken—are lies from the pit of hell.

Here's the truth: God's saving grace has removed the stains of your past, and His empowering grace gives you the capacity to fulfill everything God has in store for you . . . and your future is bright! You're redeemed from the curse of the law, with all of its demands and condemnation. That took God's saving grace. Now, you can trust God's empowering grace to give you confidence, truth, joy, and strength to be all God wants you to be. You are absolutely authorized and equipped to accomplish everything you were saved for!

In the church we may have focused too much on Christ's death and not enough on His resurrection. For this reason, people may have stopped at being forgiven and don't experience the power and presence of God in their everyday lives. The day we were saved was a huge day, but it was just the beginning, not the sum total of all God wants to do in us and through us. There's more . . . lots more.

BUT WHAT ABOUT . . .

What is it about some people? All of us have suffered from past emotional and relational wounds, and we've done things we're not proud of. A few people find God's grace to be so magnificent that their hurts are healed and their sins put in the rearview mirror. But the past consumes other people. They become self-absorbed, filled with self-pity and resentment. Here's the truth: no matter how we've struggled in the past, when we dive deeper into empowering grace, we can turn bitterness into "better-ness."

With a new identity, a new sense of hope, and a new purpose, we trust that God will use even our deepest wounds and biggest sins to display His magnificent love and power. The true testimony of grace isn't what God has delivered us from, but what He leads us to.

As a pastor, I've been thrilled when people come to Christ and are gloriously saved, but I've watched many of those people sit and worship for years without taking steps to make their lives count. It's obvious to me that they see the moment of salvation as the end, not the beginning. They need to experience God's empowering grace. I want to tell them, "If you never live in the next dimension of grace, you'll never accomplish what God has designed you to do."

The good news is that God never gives up on us. We can always choose to be sons instead of children, to be free and powerful instead of in bondage and weak. No matter who you are, what you've done, or how long you've been dormant, God has something wonderful for you.

In the early chapters of Genesis, we read the creation story, but it's a drama, not a comedy. Because Adam and Eve wanted to "be like God," they gave in to temptation and sin tainted the world. God banished them from Eden, but He wasn't finished with them. He still had a plan for their lives. The couple had two sons, Cain and Abel. When we hear their names, most of us think of Cain murdering Abel, but there's more to the story. In fact, we can draw three very practical principles from this biblical account.

First, embrace the process.

This is the lesson my dad tried to teach me when we were on our long trips in the car, and it's the lesson God wants to teach all of us. We live in a microwave culture. We can get almost anything in the blink of an eye. Modern conveniences are wonderful, but I'm afraid they erode our appreciation for the longer, slower process of spiritual development. The word *process* isn't a filthy, seven-letter word! In fact, it's an essential ingredient for living the abundant life.

Outside the Garden, God began to expand the community of human beings: "Now Adam knew Eve his wife, and she conceived and bore Cain, and said, 'I have acquired a man from the Lord.' Then she bore again, this time his brother Abel. Now Abel was a keeper of sheep, but Cain was a tiller of the ground. And in the process of time it came to pass that Cain brought an offering of the fruit of the ground to the Lord" (Genesis 4:1-3 NKJV).

We can identify three specific points about the process:

First, God always uses "the process of time." Creation is a process, childbirth is a process, the growing season involves a process, physical development is a process, and Jesus was born "when the fullness of time had come" (Galatians 4:4). How ridiculous is it to assume that we can throw some grain on the ground and expect a loaf of bread to instantly appear! But that's what many of us expect from God. We want shortcuts to spiritual maturity, but it just doesn't work that way.

God used Joseph to save his family and the nation of Egypt from starvation, but it took years of slavery and prison to position him for that role. Paul met Jesus on the road to Damascus, but he spent several years in training and preparation before he was ready to plant churches.

In fact, the "Hall of Heroes" in Hebrews 11 is a study of delays that remind us how God used difficulties to shape the lives of these leaders.

Over the years, I've been as impatient as anyone, but I've learned that the process of growth is necessary to produce certain qualities in us. For instance, the process develops character. I can't tell you how many careers of supremely gifted people in all walks of life have been derailed by character flaws. They started well, but they finished poorly. Talent may get you through the door, but character will keep you in the room.

In our impatience, it's easy to revert back to the law as our standard of development.

When grace doesn't seem to work as quickly as we hope, we take matters into our own hands. This is a deadly miscalculation. Reaping always comes after sowing, but not *immediately* after. Paul often used agrarian metaphors to make his points. His corrective letter to the Galatians was designed to put them back on track to trust in God's grace instead of their ability to keep the law, and he reminded them: "Do not be deceived, God is not mocked; for whatever a man sows, that he will also reap. For he who sows to his flesh will of the flesh reap corruption, but he who sows to the Spirit will from the Spirit reap everlasting life. And let us not grow weary while doing good, for in due season we shall reap if we do not lose heart" (Galatians 6:7-9 NKJV).

Second, the process cleans up messes. When we're in a hurry, we ignore the messes we've made in our relationships, our careers, and our characters. A commitment to the process slows us down so we can take a long, hard look at these. Cleaning out a cluttered garage seems like drudgery when we're in the middle of it, but the process gives us a sense of accomplishment. When we're finished, the people around us appreciate our tenacity, and we may just find that album we lost a couple of years ago!

Third, God often uses pressure as part of the process. In a culture that expects only pleasure and success (and expects them instantly), Christians often misunderstand God's purposes in our pain. Over the years, I've been learning that God allows delays and disappointments because He's taking me to another level in my relationship with Him.

In fact, God sometimes takes us on a journey into unbearable pressure. Just ask Job. The entire book of Job is about his wrestling with God and asking, "Why, God? Why did you let all these disasters happen?" His friends weren't any help. They blamed him! Finally, in the last chapters, God showed up. He provided an answer, but it wasn't at all what Job expected. God said, in effect, "I'm God, and you're not. There are some things you'll never understand. Just trust Me."

Paul experienced some unbearable pressures. In his second letter to the Corinthians, he listed some of them:

> I have worked much harder, been in prison more frequently, been flogged more severely, and been exposed to death again and again. Five times I received from the Jews the forty lashes minus one. Three times I was beaten with rods, once I was pelted with stones, three times I was shipwrecked, I spent a night and a day in the open sea, I have been constantly on the move. I have been in danger from rivers, in danger from bandits, in danger from my fellow Jews, in danger from Gentiles; in danger in the city, in danger in the country, in danger at sea; and in danger from false believers. I have labored and toiled and have often gone without sleep; I have known hunger and thirst and have often gone without food; I have been cold and naked. Besides everything else, I face daily the pressure of my concern for all the churches. Who is weak, and I do not

feel weak? Who is led into sin, and I do not inwardly burn? (2 Corinthians 11:23-29).

But that wasn't the worst of it! In the opening verses of the letter, Paul described another situation that was utterly unbearable: "We do not want you to be uninformed, brothers and sisters, about the troubles we experienced in the province of Asia. We were under great pressure, far beyond our ability to endure, so that we despaired of life itself. Indeed, we felt we had received the sentence of death. But this happened that we might not rely on ourselves but on God, who raises the dead" (2 Corinthians 1:8-9).

Have you ever felt that you were under such pressure that it was beyond your ability to endure . . . that you thought you were going to die? That was Paul's experience. Even then, Paul realized God was using his circumstances for good. He told them what he'd learned: "Praise be to the God and Father of our Lord Jesus Christ, the Father of compassion and the God of all comfort, who comforts us in all our troubles, so that we can comfort those in any trouble with the comfort we ourselves receive from God" (vv. 3-4).

Some people claim that "God won't let us experience anything we can't endure," and they cite 1 Corinthians 10:13 for proof, but that's not what the passage says. Paul promises that we won't endure any *temptation* we can't handle because God will give us a way out through faithful obedience, but there are plenty of instances when God allowed people to experience suffering they couldn't endure. God uses our burdens to teach us to put our total trust in Him so we stop trusting in ourselves. Then, when He acts to resolve the situation or He gives us supernatural peace to endure it, it's clear (to us and to those who are watching) that God is the source of our strength. And through the experience, we learn that we can trust Him the next time we face unbearable burdens.

What's the problem with misunderstanding the promise in 1 Corinthians 10? I've seen people draw several different painful and destructive conclusions:

- Some struggle not only with the weight of their burdens, but they suffer even more because they've been taught they're suffering because they don't have enough faith to experience victory. Guilt is piled onto their pain.

- Some have been told, like Job's friends told him, that they must have some terrible, unconfessed sin.

- And maybe the worst problem is that some people fake it and act like everything is "just fine," and they call their pretentions "faith." It's not, it's only a façade.

Paul wouldn't have chosen the classroom of unbearable burdens, but God chose it for him. Why? So he would learn more about God's love, comfort, and kindness in the middle of heartache. He had a revolutionary perspective on his suffering. Later in the second letter to the Corinthians, Paul shared the insight that God was using his "thorn in the flesh" (and I believe his thorn was the legalistic teachers who were leading people away from grace and attacking him for his message) to humble him after he had a magnificent revelation:

Because of the extravagance of those revelations, and so I wouldn't get a big head, I was given the gift of a handicap to keep me in constant touch with my limitations. Satan's angel did his best to get me down; what he in fact did was push me to my knees. No danger then of walking around high and mighty!

At first I didn't think of it as a gift, and begged God to remove it. Three times I did that, and then he told me,

> My grace is enough; it's all you need.
> My strength comes into its own in your weakness.

Once I heard that, I was glad to let it happen. I quit focusing on the handicap and began appreciating the gift. It was a case of Christ's strength moving in on my weakness. Now I take limitations in stride, and with good cheer, these limitations that cut me down to size—abuse, accidents, opposition, bad breaks. I just let Christ take over! And so the weaker I get, the stronger I become. (2 Corinthians 12:7-10 MSG)

And remember, Paul said, "Follow my example, as I follow the example of Christ" (1 Corinthians 11:1). That means we follow Paul in suffering even in times we don't understand its purpose, we follow him in trusting that God has good intentions even when we don't see them, and we follow him in seeing that admitting our weaknesses makes us dependent on God's infinite strength.

Is that what God wants us to learn, too? Certainly. In his classic book, *Knowing God*, author and professor J. I. Packer explains:

> This is what all the work of grace aims at—an ever deeper knowledge of God, and an ever closer fellowship with Him. Grace is God drawing us sinners closer and closer to Himself.
>
> How does God in grace prosecute this purpose? Not by shielding us from assault by the world, the flesh, and the devil, nor by protecting us from burdensome and frustrating circumstances, nor yet by shielding us from troubles created by our own temperament and psychology; but rather by exposing us

to all these things, so as to overwhelm us with a sense of our own inadequacy, and to drive us to cling to Him more closely. This is the ultimate reason, from our standpoint, why God fills our lives with troubles and perplexities of one sort and another—it is to ensure that we shall learn to hold Him fast. . . . They say that those who never make mistakes never make anything; certainly, these men made mistakes, but through their mistakes God taught them to know His grace, and to cleave to Him in a way that would never have happened otherwise. Is your trouble a sense of failure? The knowledge of having made some ghastly mistake? Go back to God; His restoring grace waits for you.[23]

Years ago, I read a book called *Tough Times Never Last but Tough People Do*. At the time, I believed it, but not any longer. Sometimes tough times never end, but God's love, wisdom, and power are still available to us if we'll trust Him. Actually, I'm thinking of writing a book called *Tough Times Seem to Go On and On, But Weak People Realize God's Grace Is Enough to See Them Through*. (Okay, the title is too long, but you get the idea.) God's grace doesn't erode in the storms of life. It's the rock we cling to when there's nothing else within reach. Grace is the love of God reaching down and gathering us in His arms. It's the confident assurance that with God on our side, we may suffer losses, but we'll eventually win. Grace is the power of God unleashed in the middle of our unbearable pressures. In three words, grace is *God with us*. Grace is Jesus, and Jesus is grace. We've been rescued from the jungle, and we've been captured again—but this time, by God's grace.

Second, trust and obedience position you in the flow of God's blessing.

Let's return to the story of Cain and Abel. The next two verses tell us: "Abel also brought of the firstborn of his flock and of their fat. And the Lord respected Abel and his offering, but He did not respect Cain and his offering. And Cain was very angry, and his countenance fell" (Genesis 4:4-5 NKJV). God didn't love one son over the other, but He respected the offering of one more than the other. Abel's offering was acceptable because it was the firstborn, a picture of Christ's sacrifice as the first-fruit. Abel brought his best; Cain brought something less than his best.

What do we bring to God? Do we live with a holy calling, a consuming desire to make the name of Jesus great? Is our goal to respond to the amazing grace of God and become faithful, grateful sons who live for our Father's honor? Instead of honoring God with our best, many of us are more like Cain, offering God our leftovers, but complaining that those who are acting like sons are more blessed than we are. When we have this victim mentality, we're seldom satisfied and usually resentful. You don't have to kill your brother to be in this category, but you may detest people who live as sons of the King.

Quite often, our resentment isn't even reasonable because we don't know the struggles those people have endured to grow in their faith and become mature sons. We may see their success, but we don't see their private battles. We may see their glory, but we don't know their story. We may see their harvest, but we didn't see how they plowed, sowed, watered, and weeded when no one was looking. We see their blessing, but we didn't see them pressing.

Eugene Peterson, translator of *The Message Bible*, described the Christian life as "a long obedience in the same direction."[24] We can choose to obey for many different reasons—some of which promote growth, or others that hinder it. Yes, it's certainly possible to be rigorously obedient and completely miss the heart of God. Just ask the Pharisees!

But I've seen many instances in my life and the lives of others when obedience out of gratitude resulted in overwhelming blessings from the hand of God. When we trust God and step out in faith—even when we don't want to and even when we can't see what's going to happen—we can be confident that God is with us. My dad often told me, "Ben, there's no safer place on earth than being in the place of faith and obedience."

Like Abel, bring your best to God, pursue Him and His purpose with all your heart, and watch what He does in you and through you. I guarantee that you'll hit some snags along the way, but I also guarantee that the blessings will be worth it.

And third, never give up.

I don't know if any of us can conceive of having "a bad day" like Adam and Eve had after they ate from the tree and were banished from the Garden, and few of us have experienced the excruciating agony of having one of our children murder a sibling. Yet through it all, God still had a good plan for them.

Adam and Eve lost people who were precious to them: one son was dead and the other was a fugitive. How did they respond? "And Adam knew his wife again, and she bore a son and named him Seth, 'For God has appointed another seed for me instead of Abel, whom Cain killed'" (Genesis 4:25 NKJV). Seth's name means *appointed* or *placed*. Eve understood that God had given her this son. In the midst of her anguish, she continued to trust God, and He provided.

You may have lost something precious—a marriage, a child, a great job, an opportunity, a dear friend, your health, or something equally valuable. Or maybe you've lost your sense of purpose, your direction, or your peace of mind. I'm convinced that we sell God short when we say, "He's a God of second chances," because He's actually a God of an infinite number of chances! No matter what you've lost, God is sending you a Seth. He's giving you another chance. This is your appointed time and place. Take it. Live in it. Expect God to bless you in it.

Amazingly, the story of the first family doesn't end there. In the very next verse, we read, "And as for Seth, to him also a son was born; and he named him Enosh. Then men began to call on the name of the Lord" (v. 26). In the third generation, they "began to call on the name of the Lord." The story of mankind had been going downhill, but when they faced calamity, they turned failure into success and curses into blessings. That's not the way the world operates, but it's the way of the kingdom of God. It's an upside-down kingdom.

When we're weak, we have a choice: give up in self-pity or rely on God's strength instead of our own. When we've come to the end of our own wisdom, we have a choice: to become bitter because things didn't work out the way we planned or trust that God knows far more than we do and He has us in His hands.

Seth was the second chance for Adam and Eve. The boy helped heal the hurt of losing their sons, and he offered hope for a better future when he grew up and had a son. God makes all things new!

IT'S NEVER OVER

It's my heart's desire that God will use this book to convince you of the enormous breadth of His saving grace and the unstoppable strength of His empowering grace. Keep going deeper into the truths of your legal standing and identity, and keep growing stronger through the grace God offers all day every day. Don't be afraid to admit your weakness— it's the source of your greatest strength. Don't stop at the destination of salvation. Keep pursuing God's love, wisdom, and power, and share everything you're learning with the next generation. You weren't just saved from something; you were saved for something.

On your journey, learn all you can about grace, and distinguish it from the demands and judgment of the law. Don't settle for anything less than the life-transforming experience of God's tender and powerful love. Don't let anyone convince you that you're hopeless because you've failed so badly that God has given up on you. Keep walking in the next dimension of grace. Know God, be filled with the fulness of Him, and watch Him do what only He can do in you and through you. The war is over! Grace has captured you. Come out of the jungle and live . . . really live.

DECLARATION:

God's grace is enough. It's all I need.

CONSIDER THIS:

1. Do you agree or disagree with the premise of this chapter that many Christians see their salvation experience as the end, not the beginning of the journey? Explain your answer.

2. How would you explain the connection between God's divine calling in a person's life and empowering grace?

3. What are some differences between a child and a son?

4. On a scale of 0 (not at all) to 10 (completely), how patient and persistent are you to partner with God in the process of spiritual development? Explain your answer.

5. What are some reasons people become stagnant in their walks with God? How might the story of Adam, Eve, their three sons,

and a grandson give them encouragement to keep trusting and obeying God . . . for the right reasons?

6. What are the three most important things you've learned from this book? How will you make them "sticky" in your heart and your life?

ENDNOTES

1 In his book, *The Gospel in Ten Words*, Paul Ellis tells a story from the end of World War II to illustrate the captivity that results from not believing the truth. It's such a compelling story that I want to include it here, too.

2 "The Japanese Soldier Who Kept on Fighting after WW2 Had Finished," History, https://www.history.co.uk/shows/lost-gold-of-wwii/articles/the-japanese-soldier-who-kept-on-fighting-after-ww2-had-finished

3 N. T. Wright, "The New Testament Doesn't Say What Most People Think It Does about Heaven," *Time*, December 16, 2019, https://time.com/5743505/new-testament-heaven/

4 "Post-traumatic stress disorder (PTSD)," Mayo Clinic, https://www.mayoclinic.org/diseases-conditions/post-traumatic-stress-disorder/symptoms-causes/syc-20355967

5 The concepts in this part of the chapter are adapted from Steve McVey, *52 Lies Heard in Church Every Sunday* (Eugene, Oregon: Harvest House Publishers, 2011), pp. 31-34.

6 John Newton, "We Were Once as You Are," 1779.

7 Paul Ellis, "Five ways Jesus revealed grace," February 2, 2012, escapetoreality.org/2012/02/02/jesus-reveals-what-is-grace

8 Ibid.

9 Paul Ellis, *The Gospel in Ten Words* (Auckland, New Zealand: KingsPress, 2012), p. 30.

10 Brené Brown, "Shame v. Guilt," January 14, 2013, https://brenebrown.com/blog/2013/01/14/shame-v-guilt/

11 Martin Luther, *St. Paul's Epistle to the Galatians* (Philadelphia: Smith, English & Co., 1860), 206.

12 John R. W. Stott, *Men Made New* (Downers Grove, Illinois: Inter-Varsity Fellowship, 1966), p. 47.

13 *Band of Brothers*, https://www.youtube.com/watch?v=O5YpUsDsHmk

14   Kit Yarrow, PhD, "Why 'Retail Therapy' Works," *Psychology Today*, May 2, 2013, https://www.psychologytoday.com/us/blog/the-why-behind-the-buy/201305/why-retail-therapy-works

15   N. T. Wright, *After You Believe* (New York: HarperOne, 2010), pp. 18-20.

16   Trisha Priebe, "13 Famous People who Were Adopted," LifeSong, November 1, 2017, https://lifesong.org/2017/11/13-famous-people-who-were-adopted/

17   "The Effects of Early Social-Emotional and Relationship Experience on the Development of Young Orphanage Children," Health and Human Services, National Institutes of Health, https://www.ncbi.nlm.nih.gov/pmc/articles/PMC2702123/

18   Joseph Mattera, "11 Contrasting Traits between an Orphan Spirit and a Spirit of Sonship," March 16, 2017, https://josephmattera.org/eleven-contrasting-traits-between-an-orphan-spirit-and-a-spirit-of-sonship/

19   Arlie Russell Hochschild, *Strangers in Their Own Land* (New York: The New York Press, 2016), pp. xii, 6.

20   Arthur S. Meintjes, *Knowing and Experiencing God* (South Africa: Kingdom Life Ministries Publications, 2005), pp. 235-237.

21   Virginia Stem Owens, "God and Man at Texas A&M," *Reformed Journal* 37, no. 11 (1987), pp. 3–4.

22   Dan Stone and David Gregory, *The Rest of the Gospel* (Eugene, Oregon: Harvest House Publishers, 2000), p. 181.

23   J. I. Packer, *Knowing God* (Downers Grove: Illinois: InterVarsity Press, 1973), pp. 226-228.

24   Eugene Peterson, *A Long Obedience in the Same Direction* (Downers Grove, Illinois: InterVarsity Press, 2000).

USING *CAPTURED BY GRACE* IN GROUPS AND CLASSES

This book is designed for individual study, small groups, and classes. The best way to absorb and apply these principles is for each person to individually study and answer the questions at the end of each chapter then to discuss them in either a class or a group environment.

Each chapter's questions are designed to promote reflection, application, and discussion. Order enough copies of the book for each person to have a copy. For couples, encourage both to have their own book so they can record their individual reflections.

A recommended schedule for a small group or class might be:

WEEK 1

Introduce the material. As a group leader, tell your story of finding and fulfilling God's dream, share your hopes for the group, and provide books for each person. Encourage people to read the assigned chapter each week and answer the questions.

WEEKS 2–11

Each week, introduce the topic for the week and share a story of how God has used the principles in your life. In small groups, lead people through a discussion of the questions at the end of the chapter. In classes, teach the principles in each chapter, use personal illustrations, and invite discussion.

PERSONALIZE EACH LESSON

Don't feel pressured to cover every question in your group discussions. Pick out three or four that had the biggest impact on you, and focus on those, or ask people in the group to share their responses to the questions that meant the most to them that week.

Make sure you personalize the principles and applications. At least once in each group meeting, add your own story to illustrate a particular point.

Make the Scriptures come alive. Far too often, we read the Bible like it's a phone book, with little or no emotion. Paint a vivid picture for people. Provide insights about the context of people's encounters with God, and help those in your class or group sense the emotions of specific people in each scene.

FOCUS ON APPLICATION

The questions at the end of each chapter and your encouragement to group members to be authentic will help your group take big steps to apply the principles they're learning. Share how you are applying the principles in particular chapters each week, and encourage them to take steps of growth, too.

THREE TYPES OF QUESTIONS

If you have led groups for a few years, you already understand the importance of using open questions to stimulate discussion. Three types of questions are *limiting, leading,* and *open.* Many of the questions at the end of each lesson are open questions.

Limiting questions focus on an obvious answer, such as, "What does Jesus call Himself in John 10:11?" They don't stimulate reflection or discussion. If you want to use questions like these, follow them with thought-provoking, open questions.

Leading questions require the listener to guess what the leader has in mind, such as, "Why did Jesus use the metaphor of a shepherd in John 10?" (He was probably alluding to a passage in Ezekiel, but many people don't know that.) The teacher who asks a leading question has a definite answer in mind. Instead of asking this kind of question, you should just teach the point and perhaps ask an open question about the point you have made.

Open questions usually don't have right or wrong answers. They stimulate thinking, and they are far less threatening because the person answering doesn't risk ridicule for being wrong. These questions often begin with "Why do you think…?" or "What are some reasons that…?" or "How would you have felt in that situation?"

PREPARATION

As you prepare to teach this material in a group or class, consider these steps:

1. Carefully and thoughtfully read the book. Make notes, highlight key sections, quotes, or stories, and complete the reflection section at the end of each chapter. This will familiarize you with the entire scope of the content.

2. As you prepare for each week's class or group, read the corresponding chapter again and make additional notes.

3. Tailor the amount of content to the time allotted. You won't have time to cover all the questions, so pick the ones that are most pertinent.

4. Add your own stories to personalize the message and add impact.

5. Before and during your preparation, ask God to give you wisdom, clarity, and power. Trust Him to use your group to change people's lives.

6. Most people will get far more out of the group if they read the chapter and complete the reflection each week. Order books before the group or class begins or after the first week.

ABOUT THE AUTHOR

Ben Dailey is the Lead Pastor of Calvary Church, a multi-locational church based in the DFW Metroplex. He is known for his love for the gospel, his creative style of communication, and his unconventional ministry. He oversees one of the most culturally diverse congregations in the nation. Ben's unique approach to ministry is paired with a genuine love for people, which produces an atmosphere conducive to heart transformation.

Ben is the author of *Collide: When Your Desires Meet God's Heart* and *Limitless: The Life You Were Meant to Live.* He has also served as a church planter and ministry consultant.

Ben oversees Gospel Circle of Churches and Ministries, which is a relational onramp to both Calvary Church and Ben Dailey Ministries. He also oversees Gospel Institute, a New Covenant education program.

Ben and his wife Kim have been married for twenty-seven years. They have three children, Kyla and Marcy (their son-in-law who is like one of their kids) and Kade, who also love serving at Calvary Church.

RESOURCES

To order these books, go to BenDailey.com

COLLIDE

To some degree, all of us have faulty assumptions about God and life. We want it all—and we think we deserve it all. Sooner or later, we get a wake-up call. Our desires collide with God's heart, and we realize His purposes are far bigger than we ever dreamed. When the collision occurs, we realize we've been wrong about many things. At that moment, we have a choice: Will we walk away from God, shake our fist at Him, or cling to Him like never before?

A collision with God's heart isn't the end of our life's dream. It's the beginning.

LIMITLESS

The relentless, unwavering grace of God is staggering. It blows up your misunderstanding, your false pride, and your secret fears. In *Limitless*, Ben Dailey reminds you that when you focus on God's grace, His amazing love will destroy your fears. You'll learn to accept that despite the cataclysmic disruption caused by sin, God has never given up on you. Through *Limitless*, you'll remember that you don't need to earn His love through duty nor do you need to try and prove yourself.

Simply receive it, bask in it, and let it change you from the inside out. Allow Jesus to fill your heart with an ocean of His love, forgiveness, and acceptance.

GOSPEL CIRCLE
OF CHURCHES + MINISTRIES

Gospel Circle of Churches and Ministries (GCCM) is more than a network. It is a relational onramp to both Calvary Church and Ben Dailey designed to bring support and solutions to your church and ministry.

GCCM's foundation is one of a kind, in that it is built purely and uniquely on a gospel-centered, New Covenant approach to church, ministry, and community. All other areas of GCCM flow from this foundational value.

For more information, go to GCCM.cc

GOSPEL INSTITUTE

Gospel Institute is a ministry of Calvary Church, a multi-locational church based in the Dallas/Ft. Worth Metroplex. Gospel Institute is a 10-course New Covenant education, focusing on the spiritual realm, the realm of faith—what God knows to be true about us. Through a variety of courses, taught by a diverse and accomplished group of New Covenant instructors from across the country, students will grow in God's grace and intimacy with Jesus to move beyond the understanding of saving grace to empowering grace. Gospel Institute will prepare students to lead in their local churches and communities.

For more information, go to GospelInstitute.cc